THE RIDDLE OF CANTINFLAS

THE RIDDLE
OF CANTINFLAS

**ESSAYS ON HISPANIC
POPULAR CULTURE**

Ilan Stavans

UNIVERSITY OF NEW MEXICO PRESS: ALBUQUERQUE

Books by Ilan Stavans in English

Fiction
The One-Handed Pianist and Other Stories

Nonfiction
Art and Anger: Essays on Politics and the Imagination
Bandido
The Hispanic Condition
Imagining Columbus: The Literary Voyage

Editor
The Oxford Book of Latin American Essays
New World
Tropical Synagogues: Short Stories by Jewish-Latin American Writers
Growing Up Latino: Memoirs and Stories
(co-edited with Harold Augenbraum)

Translation
Sentimental Songs by Felipe Alfau

The essays in this collection first appeared, in somewhat different form, in the following publications: "Santa Selena" in *The New Republic*; "Hanukkah: A Brief Reminiscence" in *Sí Magazine*; "Unmasking Marcos," "The Riddle of Cantinflas," and "How Hispanics Became Brown" in *Transition*; "Frida and Benita: Unparalleled Lives" as the preface to *Benita Galeana* (Latin American Literary Review Press, 1994); "Carlos Fuentes in His Labyrinth," "Strawberry and Chocolate," and "Laura Esquivel's Second Act" in *In These Times*; "José Guadalupe Posada" in the *Journal of Decorative and Propaganda Arts*; "Sandra Cisneros: Form Over Content" in *Academic Questions*; "Borderland: A Letter" *in Review: Latin American Literature and Arts*; "Appeal of the False *Quixote*" in *La pluma y la máscara* (Fondo de Cultura Económica, 1993) and, in English translation, in *The Bloomsbury Review*; "Like a Bride" and "A Kiss to This Land" in the 1995 catalogue of the Boston Jewish Film Festival; "Sam Spade, *Otra Vez*," "Señora Rodríguez's Purse," "*Tinísima*," "Like Water for Chocolate," "*Buffalo Nickel*," "Rosario Ferré's Macondo," "Autumn of the Matriarch," and "Melodrama *á la cubana*" in *The Nation*.

Library of Congress Cataloging-in-Publication Data
Stavans, Ilan
The riddle of Cantinflas: essays on Hispanic popular culture / Ilan Stavans.—1st ed.
p.   cm. Includes index.
ISBN 0-8263-1860-6 (cloth), ISBN 0-8263-1925-4 (paper)
1. Popular culture—Latin America. 2. Kitsch—Latin America. 3. Cantinflas, 1911–   . I. Title.
F1408.3.S73 1998
306'.098—dc21
97–39726
CIP

CONTENTS

	Illustrations	vi
	Preface	vii
1.	Santa Selena	3
2.	Hanukkah: A Brief Reminiscence	10
3.	Unmasking Marcos	13
4.	Sam Spade, *otra vez*	25
5.	The Riddle of Cantinflas	31
6.	Frida and Benita: Unparalleled Lives	53
7.	Carlos Fuentes in His Labyrinth	57
8.	José Guadalupe Posada: A Profile	63
9.	Señora Rodríguez's Purse	76
10.	Sandra Cisneros: Form Over Content	81
11.	*Tinísima*	89
12.	Films	94
13.	Laura Esquivel's Second Act	109
14.	Borderland: A Letter	114
15.	*Buffalo Nickel*	117
16.	Appeal of the False *Quixote*	122
17.	Rosario Ferré's Macondo	125
18.	Autumn of the Matriarch	129
19.	How Hispanics Became Brown	135
20.	Melodrama á la cubana	148
	Index	153

ILLUSTRATIONS

Day of the Dead remembrance of Selena 2

Subcomandante Marcos 14

*Zapatista Action Figures, San Cristóbal, Chiapas,
Mexico* 17

Miguel Covarrubias, *Cantinflas*, ca. 1937 30

Dolores Camarillo "Fraustita" and Cantinflas,
from *Ahí está el detalle* 43

Poster of *Ahi está el detalle* 44

José Guadalupe Posada, *¡Caso raro! Una mujer
que dio a luz tres niños y cuatro animales* 65

José Guadalupe Posada, *Esta es de Don Quijote
la primera, la sin par, la gigante calavera* 67

Tina Modotti, *El machete* 88

Still from *Like a Bride* 99

Publicity photo from *A Kiss to This Land* 101

Poster of *A Kiss to This Land* 102

Cover of *Como agua para Chocolate* 111

PREFACE

Kitsch is king in the Hispanic world. Nothing is original and all things are their own parody. I say this not in a condescending tone: counterfeit is beautiful. The region is hypnotizing in its artificiality; everything in it is bogus: the Roman alphabet is, in and of itself, an extraneous import, and so life must be lived in translation; likewise, democracy, condoms, Aristotle, TV soaps, clocks, blackness, money, violins, Satan, and antibiotics are all foreign idols. No wonder its citizens aren't skilled at producing but at reproducing.

In fact, kitsch, as a concept, must be fully and painstakingly redefined so as to capture its immense possibilities south of the Rio Grande. Clement Greenberg believed it to be a counterpoint to bohemian art. "Where there is an avant-garde," he would argue, "generally we also find a rearguard . . . that thing to which Germans give the wonderful name of *Kitsch*: popular, commercial art and literature with their chromeotypes, magazine covers, illustrations, ads, slick and pulp fiction, Hollywood movies, etc., etc." Walter Benjamin saw it as the automatic attempt to turn a one into a many, of making uniqueness into multiplicity. But these views apply solely to Europe and the United States, where kitsch, "that gigantic apparition," is a mass-made product. In the modern Latin American orbit, though, it encompasses much more: high- and low-brow culture and middle-brow as well; the masses and the elite; the unique and the duplicated—in short, the entire culture. Everything in the region is slick, everything a postcard, everything a never-ending et cetera, including, of course, those manifestations striving to be pure and authentic at heart and designed to repel all foreign influences. What is its population without these foreign influences?

All this leads one to conclude that the triumphant entrance of kitsch into history did not come about, as Greenberg falsely believed, with the rapid population growth that affected the industrialized nations in the first third of our century. Nor was it born, as Benjamin misstated in "The Work of Art in the Age of Mechanical Reproduction," when photography became a fashion in France and Germany. Instead, the origins of kitsch are to be found elsewhere; they are a product of the Spanish mediocrity, of its frivolity. Yes, honor to whom honor is due. If Spain can pride itself of any solid contribution to Western civilization, it is precisely that derivativeness, that hand-me-downness practiced from generation to generation light years before the Xerox machine was even invented. Only within its national borders is the art of copying, of imitating, a national sport, and it is apparent in all epochs, from the massively produced chivalry novels that accompanied the Iberian conquistadors in the colonization of the so-called New World, to Pedro Almodóvar's fashionable *cursilería*. Kitsch, in Western eyes, carries along a sense of fraudulence, of sin, of imposture, of plagiarism, but not in Spain, where talent must be found in the lack of talent, where fantasy is congenital to the trite and repetitive. What is *Don Quixote* if not first-rate art born from exhaustion and duplication? How to explain the Spanish Golden Age if not by invoking Lope de Vega's 728 "original" *comedias*? What is baroque architecture if not a caricature of previous architectural modes? In fact, I am tempted to date with as much precision as is advisable—and I do so in "Appeal of the False *Quixote*"—the moment when kistch became an inseparable stamp of the Hispanic idiosyncrasy: in 1614, when Avellaneda, trying to beat a turtle-paced Cervantes, appropriated the characters of Don Quixote and Sancho and published the second part of *Don Quixote*. The age of illegitimacy was thus legitimated.

Analogously, the Americas, an outgrowth of Spain, are a sequel, an imitation of an imitation, a plagiarist plagiarizing another plagiarist, Velázquez's Meninas within Velázquez's Meninas. No wonder Simón Bolívar dreamt of becoming a South American Napoleon; no wonder the first modern novel in Spanish America, *The Itching Parrot* by Fernández de Lizardi, was modeled after *El lazarillo de Tormes*; no wonder Cubans are called "the Jews of the Caribbean"; no wonder Benito

Juárez is the Mexican Abraham Lincoln; no wonder Buenos Aires is London-on-the-River-Plate; and no wonder Pierre Menard rewrites *Don Quixote*—that is, he doesn't set out to copy it verbatim, but simply to *re*compose it from memory, word by word and comma by comma. To *re*compose, to *re*create, to *re*vive. . . . If Spaniards are semimodels, Latin Americans are hypermodels, countermodels, and antimodels: Frida Kahlo's pure fake becomes a myth; Selena's virginal beauty is a hybrid, an in-between confused with the *Vírgen de Guadalupe*; Subcomandante Marcos is not a freedom-fighter but an actor; Cantinflas is Charlie Chaplin without conscience. Nothing is real but the surreal.

I have been infatuated by this duplicity, by this all-encompassing artificiality, for quite some time. Its possibilities seem to me infinite. If asked to explain the reason behind my obsession, I am tempted to reply that I am myself a double-*entendre*, a bit Jewish and a bit Hispanic and, lately, a bit American as well, neither here nor there—a faked self. The reply might not be convincing enough, but at least it insinuates what I've said elsewhere: that I live my life possessed by the feeling that others before me have already done the same things I do, that I am but a replica. So why do *I* matter? What are my role and purpose? To call attention to this deception, perhaps, to unveil this trickery only to find out, of course, that I am both the veil and the veiled, the searcher and the object of my search. In the present volume I have collected explorations of the ins and outs of kitsch-as-life in the Hispanic world. Beware of looking for sequence, cohesiveness, and conclusiveness in these pieces, though; they are but fragmentary sketches of my intellectual curiosity, germane to the culture they emerge from. Also, as a token of self-referentiality I have reprinted a couple of short reminiscences that show the fashion in which I myself become unadulterated kitsch—an image in the image.

THE RIDDLE OF CANTINFLAS

Day of the Dead remembrance of Selena, photo by Barbara Laing.

SANTA SELENA

Saint, n. A dead sinner revised and edited.

Ambrose Bierce, The Devil's Dictionary

During a recent trip to South Texas, a dignified old man told me Selena had died because heaven was desperate for another cherub. He described her to me as "a celestial beauty whose time on earth was spent helping the poor and unattended." In San Antonio, a mother of four has placed Selena's photograph in a special altar in her home, surrounded by candles and flowers, just beneath the image of the Virgin of Guadalupe. "Please, Selena," her prayer goes, "let me remain a virgin . . . just like you." (This despite the fact that, at the time of her death, Selena was married to Chris Pérez, her guitar player.) The collective imagination is stronger than anything reality has to offer: a young lady from Corpus Christi who spends a good portion of her days singing "selenatas" swears she sees the singer's ghost appear on her TV screen every night— after she's switched the set off. And a Spanish teacher I know in Dallas who recently lost her job has begun selling a poem of her own creation, "Adiós mi linda estrella," to make money. She sent me a copy of the poem, a tribute to the pop star she considers her angel protector:

> *Do not cry for me, do not suffer for me*
> *Remember I love you with all my heart*
> *I know if you listen and do as I ask*
> *I will be content because*
> *I have completed my mission here on my beautiful earth*
>   *and*
> *I can continue to sing to Our Father in Heaven.*
> *Listen, Heaven does not thunder*
> *The sun begins to hide*

> *Our father has given us a new light*
> *Look up to Heaven*
> *The light comes from a divine star*
> *That lights up all of Heaven*
> *It is the Angel Selena*
> *The most beautiful star of the world*
> *and now of Heaven.*
> *Goodbye, my lovely Star.*

Welcome to *la frontera,* the painful wound dividing Mexico and the United States, a land of kitsch and missed opportunities where outlandish dreams and work-a-day life intertwine. Encompassing 12 million people, its capital is Tijuana, where *el día de los muertos* is the most popular holiday: an opportunity for the living to spend a wild night carousing in the cemetery at the side of their dearly departed. The flag of the region is red, white, and blue, but at its heart is an eagle devouring a writhing snake. *La frontera* is where NAFTA and Kafka cohabit, where English isn't spoken but broken, and where *yo* becomes *I,* and where *I* becomes *Ay, carajo*—a free zone, autonomous and self-referential, perceived by Mexicans as *el fin del mundo,* and by Anglo-Americans as a galaxy of bad taste.

Since her tragic death, Selena has become omnipresent in *la frontera,* the focal point of a collective suffering—a patron saint, of sorts. Tender *señoritas* cannot bring themselves to accept the idea that she is no longer with us. On radio call-in shows, her followers bemoan the injustice of her disappearance. A movie is in the works, several instant biographies have already been published (in Spanish and English), and more are on their way to the printer. Countless imitators mimic her style, her idiosyncratic fashion, her smile: an upcoming national contest in Corpus Christi will soon crown the girl who impersonates Selena most perfectly, who loses herself in Selena's chaste yet sexy persona. In fact, the whole of Lake Jackson, Texas, Selena's hometown, has already become a kind of Graceland: pilgrims come to weep at her birth place, and to pay homage at the places she graced with her presence: her home, the neighborhood rodeos where she sang at intermission, the arenas where she entertained the masses. Her grave at Seaside Memorial Park is inundated daily with flowers, candles, and mementos, and the cemetery keeper has trouble disposing of the colorful offerings. Amalia González, a radio host in Los Angeles, says Selena had sojourned on earth in order "to unite all creeds and races."

Elvis, John Lennon, Kurt Cobain, and Jerry Garcia . . . roll over: there's a new kid in the pop star firmament, one who gives voice to the silenced and the oppressed. This until-yesterday unknown *tejana,* née Selena Quintanilla Pérez—awarded the Grammy for Best Mexican American Performance for an album titled, ironically, *Selena Live*—has instantly become the unquestioned queen of *mestizo* pop, part wetback and part *gabacha.*

Selena's life may have been tragically short, but death has given her an imposing stature. At 1:05 P.M. on Friday, March 31, 1995, she became immortal: just short of her twenty-fourth birthday, she ceased to exist as a pop singer of modest means but high ambitions, poised to cross over to a mainstream market, and became not only Madonna's most fearsome competitor (her album *Dreaming of You,* which included a handful of songs in English, sold 175,000 copies in a single day), but also a cult hero, a Hispanic Marilyn Monroe, an object of relentless adoration and adulation. Magically, she has joined Eva Perón in the pantheon of mystical and magical *hispanas,* protectors of the *descamisados,* immaculate personification of eternal love.

How many of us from outside *la frontera* had heard of her before the murder? Not many. But even if we had heard some of her songs on the radio, we could not have fathomed her appeal: her music is *cursi*—melodramatic, cheesy, overemotional. Tejano rhythms, which Selena was in the process of reinventing, are a jumbled fusion of rock, jazz, pop, and country, seasoned with a hint of rap—an endless addition resulting in a subtraction. She was beginning to master them all when she died. But that's not the point: her *conjunto* pieces, as well as the mental imbalances of Yolanda Saldívar, the administrator of her fan club and her killer, are only props in a theatrical act in which Selena is the star regardless of her talents. She was a symbol, not a genius.

Selena's father, Abraham Quintanilla, Jr., whose family has been in South Texas for at least a hundred years, forced her to learn Spanish in order to further her career. She debuted at age five with Los Dinos, her father's group. (He was a vocalist.) Less than twenty years later, with a sexy public persona built around a halter top and tight pants, she was worth more than $5 million. Since she passed just as her crossover dreams were beginning to materialize, her legend was never—will never—be forced to confront the conundrum of assimilation: she will go down as a brave, courageous chicana—perhaps ambivalent toward, but never ashamed of, her background. "You'd see her shopping at the Mall," people in South Texas say, wistfully. "And you'd see her working at home. A real sweetheart." Some even recalled how accessible she was—*una de nosotros:* Selena never turned up her nose at Mexican popular entertainment, performing in variety shows like *Siempre en Domingo* and the melodramatic soap *Dos mujeres, un camino,* starring Erik Estrada. Small parts, no doubt, but the real *sabor.* Had Selena been visited by the angel of death only a few years later, it would have been a very different story: she would have been an American star, and her tragedy would not serve to highlight the plight of *la frontera.*

Now Selena is ubiquitous: on TV screens and CDs, on book covers and calendars, on velvet slippers and plastic bracelets, on shampoo bottles and make-up advertisements, on designer clothes and *piñatas.* She is a present-day Frida Kahlo: a martyr whose afterlife *en el más allá* promises to be infinitely more resonant than whatever she managed to achieve *en el más acá.* In *la frontera,* she has been made into a heroine, an ethnic mass-market artifact. "Thanks to her *tejanos* are being heard," a disk-jockey from Houston told me. "She put us in the news—and on the front page." And so she did: Rosa López was merely a bit of Hispanic seasoning in the O.J. Simpson mix, but Selena has turned *la frontera—* whose children, adopted and otherwise, include film director Robert "El Mariachi" Rodríguez, performance artist Guillermo Gómez-Peña, and novelists Laura Esquivel and Cormac McCarthy—into a banquet of possibilities for the media. The trial and sentencing of Saldívar alone has catapulted Selena to eternity, winning more newspaper columns for Latinos than the Zapatista rebellion. Even Texas Governor George W. Bush, whose knowledge of *tejano* culture is close to nil, was quick enough to declare April 16, 1995—Selena's birthday and Easter Sunday—*el día de Selena.* There's even a motion to put her face on a postage stamp.

Selena's was a life quilted by sheer coincidence but which, studied in retrospect, shows the deliberate design of a well-patterned tapestry. The murder itself (which, strangely, took place on César Chávez's birthday) is already legendary, rivaling the Crucifixion for pathos and histrionics: Saldívar—whose much-lauded punishment is life in prison—comes out of Room 158 of the Corpus Christi Days Inn on Navigation Boulevard with a .38-caliber revolver. Selena stumbles ahead of her, wounded, bleeding, and crying for help. She names her assassin and then dies, in close-up. Cut! Roll the commercial. The next scene takes place minutes later, as Saldívar seals herself in a pickup truck and, holding the pistol to her temple *á la* O.J., threatens to commit suicide and keeps the police at a standstill for nine and a half hours. Blood, tears, desperation—the recipe lacks not a single ingredient. Saldívar had been a good friend of the singer and her business partner in Selena, Inc., the company which managed the singer's boutiques and beauty salons in Corpus Christi and San Antonio. So what went wrong?

You might find the answer in cyberspace, where a Selena home page on the World Wide Web has kept her *admiradores* up to date since a few weeks after her death. Or simply tune in to *El Show de Cristina,* the Spanish-speaking Oprah Winfrey, which was among the first TV programs to capitalize on Selena's tragedy by devoting several episodes to her family's sorrows. Or you might give up on investigating the logic and become a *selenomaníaco* and start building up your pile of collectibles: nightgowns, hats, purses, money holders, sleepers, umbrellas and a lot more—all sporting her beautiful photograph. Or, if you are ready for a deeper investment, keep in mind the seventy-six page special issue of *People,* which retailed at $3.95 and now sells for more than two hundred dollars. There is also, of course, the notorious April 17, 1995, issue of the same magazine, which appeared in two different versions: 442,000 copies with Selena on the cover, for sale in Texas, and 3 million issues (featuring the cast of the TV show *Friends*) for the rest of the country. A single copy of *that* Selena issue has auctioned for over $500. My own favorite item is the advertisement for the colorful T-shirt on sale at Selena, Inc. ($10.99), which is marketed as a sign of loyalty: "Tell the world of your love for Selena and her music with one of several full-color designs." One size fits all.

For those inclined to read more about it, an illustrated tribute to *La Virgen Selena* is now available, complete with photos of her grave, third-grade class, and mourning mother, plus a snapshot of the singer and her killer cavorting at a fan club appreciation party at the Desperado's Club in San Antonio during the Tejano Music Awards in 1993. Or you might want to bring home the most complete of Selena's thirteen biographies (at this writing), titled *Selena: Como la Flor* and written by Joe Nick Patoski, a senior editor at *Texas Monthly* and co-author of the bestseller *Stevie Ray Vaughan: Caught in the Crossfire.* Patoski's definitive report on the life of *la reina* will tell you how many hours a day she exercised to keep up her figure, the names of her favorite stores, the shoes she was wearing at the time of her death, and all the skinny you will never find in *The National Enquirer.* The newspaper's anti-Hispanic bias has forced its editors to ignore Selena's story from A to Z.

Never fear: Selena will survive all aggressions, and her apotheosis is not yet complete. That apex will most surely be reached with the release of the Hollywood movie by director Gregory Nava (who brought you *El Norte,* a film about the plight of poor Guatemalan immigrants in *el otro lado,* as well as *La Familia,* a transgenerational melodrama to end all melodramas). From the moment Selena's body hit the hotel floor, a pitched battle has raged over securing the movie rights to her story. (Patoski devotes several pages of his biography to the wrangling.) By all accounts, her father is firmly in command of choosing the screenwriter and, more important, who gets to play his daughter. (He also chooses who gets to play himself; unidentified sources claim that he rejected Edward James Olmos as too ugly). Selena will surely do wonders for Nava's career. She has already granted so many miracles—one more shouldn't be a problem. Victor Villaseñor is next in line for redemption, a Chicano writer known for his *Roots*-esque family epic, *Rain of Gold,* who is under contract to write the "official" companion to the film. Although the second book of his family saga was almost unreadable, it will be hard to go wrong with Selena for inspiration.*

* As it turned out, Olmos did get to play the father and Villaseñor was eliminated as screenwriter. Selena, *the movie released in 1997, was so saccharine it didn't even have a murder sequence.*

Inspiration is what she is all about. Just when Latinos were convinced no one cared for them, along came Selena. As long as *la frontera* remains a hybrid territory, hidden from the sight of Anglo America and ignored by the Mexican government, people north and south of the Rio Grande will continue to pray to their new Madonna. They have realized that the best way to conquer the mainstream culture of the United States is by media storm, a subversion from within. They are confident that sooner rather than later all *gringos* will make room for Latino extroversion and sentimentality. Sooner, rather than later, *The National Enquirer* will publish a report on her return to earth in a UFO. A new, darker-complected Elvis is here to capture the imagination of a nation: SELENA IS ALIVE.

[1996]

HANUKKAH:
A BRIEF REMINISCENCE

Hanukkah in *Distrito Federal* was a season of joy and reflection. The week-long festival of light was celebrated not only at home and in school but also, indirectly, in our Gentile neighborhood as part of the season of *posadas.* It would almost always fall several weeks before Christmas, so I have plentiful memories that unite Judas Maccabee with colorful piñatas, filled with oranges, *colación,* and bite-size pieces of sugar cane. In Yiddish school we performed humorous theater *shpiels,* patriotic in tone and spirit, re-enacting the plight of the Hasmoneans, who staged a guerrilla war in Palestine in 165 B.C.E. when the Syrian ruler Antiochus IV stripped and desecrated Jerusalem's Holy Temple. In my mind, the Jewish resistance was a mirror of the kind of uprising South American left-wing commandantes were famous for orchestrating in, say, Bolivia, El Salvador, and Nicaragua; I would imagine the Hasmoneans as freedom-fighters dressed in army fatigues and using Uzis. In fact, I remember playing Antiochus once, a role I thoroughly enjoyed, and also once Judas's father, Mattathias of Modin, a man with a beard very much like Fidel Castro's. As Antiochus I dressed like a Spanish conquistador and, simulating the voice of Presidente Luis Echeverría Alvarez, I pretended to conquer the temple, designed after the pyramid of the sun in Teotihuacán. At the end of the play we all sang classic Hebrew songs like *Hanerot Hallalu, Maoz Tsur,* and *Hava Narima,* but in the style of ranchero ballads, sounding like El Mariachi Vargas de Tecalitlán, and using verbal puns to satirize Mexico's political life. In the early evening, my parents would give me and my siblings our presents (I still remember a beautiful *títere,* a puppet of a humble campesino with huge mustache, a bottle in one hand and a pistol in the other), and then we would light another one of the candles in the menorah, placing the candelabra in the dining room window sill. Occasionally, our extended family gathered at my grandmother's house in Colonia Hipódromo, where the cousins sat in circles spinning the *dreidl,* a little top on which we gambled our Hanukkah money. (I remember that no matter how much I prayed for a miracle like the one that swept the Maccabees to redemption, I would never get the winning letter and so, at the end of the evening I would be left with no assets to speak of and a bad temper.) After the game, as we would on other Jewish holidays like Rosh Hashanah and Yom Kippur, we ate a Mexican meal, with Grandma's inevitable *pescado a la veracruzana,* chicken soup with *kneidlach,* the over-fried *latkes* accompanied by *mole poblano* and apple sauce, and, by way of dessert, delicious pastries that attempted to invoke the baking style of Eastern European Jewry but were really autochthonous *bizcochos.* As if this was not enough, at the end of the day we were often invited to join neighbors in their *posadas,* and at this point, as I recall, numerous theological questions about the meaning of Hanukkah and Judaism in general were asked by our gentile acquaintances: Why eight candles? someone would ask. Did we personally kill Jesus Christ? Did we consider Him the messiah? Searching for replies often left me with a bizarre, uncomfortable aftertaste. No, I had not killed Jesus, and neither did we consider him a Messiah. He is, my parents would state, another prophet of biblical dimensions, and a nationalistic one at that. But our Gentile friends would not take these answers at face value. Their facial gestures evidenced puzzlement. They liked us, no doubt, and perhaps a few even loved us—but we were clearly from another planet.

I only attached the term *exotic* to my Hanukkah when I emigrated to Manhattan and described these fiestas to non-Yiddish-speaking American Jewish friends whose knowledge of the Hispanic world is limited to a couple of novels by Gabriel García Márquez, to Don Francisco's popular TV show, and to short trips to the touristy beaches of Acapulco. What did strike me as singular about the holiday while still a child was that it belonged not only to me, a Mexican Jew, but to an endless chain of generations. My parents and teachers had made me an integral part of a small transnational and multilingual group—unique, abstract, marginal—dispersed in different corners of the globe and alive for many centuries. Millions of kids before me had spun the *dreidl* on this holiday and millions more would do so in many years to come. I saw myself as a passing bridge, a peon, a crucial component in an infinite chain. The accident of my Hispanic birth had only added a different cultural flavor to the already plentiful gallery of childhood smiles. I was, all Jewish children are, time-traveling Maccabees reenacting a cosmic festival of self-definition. This thought made me stronger, a superhero of sorts, a freedom-fighter with a mission: to smile was to remember, to insert myself in history.

[1996]

UNMASKING MARCOS*

Tout révolutionnaire finit en oppresseur ou en hérétique.

Albert Camus

The Subcomandante Insurgente Marcos, or *El Sup,* as he is known in Mexico. His skin is bleached, whiter than that of his compañeros. He speaks with palpable erudition. The sword *and* the pen: he is a rebel, yes, but also an intellectual, a mind perpetually alert. And like some ranting dissenter, he is always prepared to say *No: No* to five centuries of abuse of the indigenous people of Chiapas and the nearby Quintana Roo in the Yucatán Peninsula. *No* to the sclerotic one-party state that has mortgaged Mexico and her people for generations, and for generations to come.

No, No, and *No.*

El Sup is also like Sisyphus, or possibly like Jesus Christ: he bears on his shoulders an impossible burden, the aspirations and demands of an embattled people. He must know, in his heart, that the rock is too heavy, the hill too steep; his efforts will change very little in the way people go about their lives south of the Tortilla Curtain. His real task, the best he can do, is to call attention to the misery of miserable men and women.

He isn't a terrorist but a freedom fighter, and a peaceable one at that. He took up arms because debate is unfruitful in his milieu. He is a *guerrillero* for the nineties who understands, better than most people, the power of word and image. He uses allegories and anecdotes, old saws and folk tales, to convey his message. Not a politician but a story-teller— an icon knowledgeable in iconography, the new art of war, a pupil of

---

* *This essay originated in the last installment of "Mexico: Four Dispatches" in* Art and Anger: Essays on Politics and the Imagination *(Albuquerque: University of New Mexico Press, 1996).*

13

Subcomandante Marcos, photo by Jack Kurtz, Impact Visuals.

Marshall McLuhan. As he himself once wrote, "My job is to make wars by writing letters."

El Sup is a tragic hero, a Moses without a Promised Land. He stands in a long line of Latin American guerrilla heroes, at once real and mythical, an insurrectionary tradition stretching back nearly half a millennium. Figures like the legendary Enriquillo, who orchestrated an uprising among aborigines in La Española around 1518, about whom Fray Bartolomé de Las Casas writes eloquently in his *Historia de las Indias.* And Enriquillo's children: Emiliano Zapata; Augusto César Sandino, the inspiration for Daniel Ortega and the Sandinistas; Simón Bolivar, the revolutionary strategist who liberated much of South America from Spanish rule and who dreamed in the 1820s of La Gran Colombia, a republic of republics that would serve as an Hispanic mirror to the United States of America; Tupac Amaru, the Peruvian Indian leader of an unsuccessful revolt against the Iberians in 1780, whose example still inspires the Maoists in Peru; Edén Pastora, *Comandante Cero,* an early Sandinista guerrillero turned dissenter; and, of course, Fidel Castro and Ernesto "Ché" Guevara. A robust tradition of revolutionaries, overpopulated by runaway slaves, *indios, subversivos,* muralists, and disenfranchised middle-class intellectuals.

El Sup: newspaper columnists and union organizers credit him for the wake-up call that changed Mexico forever. He had gone to Chiapas in 1983 to politicize people. "We started talking to the communities, who taught us a very important lesson," he told an interviewer. "The democratic organization or social structure of the indigenous communities is very honest, very clear." He fought hard to be accepted, and he was, although his pale skin marked him as an outsider. (Though the preeminent spokesman of the Zapatista movement, he could never aspire to a position greater than subcommandante, as the highest leadership positions are customarily reserved for Indians.) The next ten years were spent mobilizing peasants, reeducating them and being reeducated in turn. The rest, as they say, is history.

And rightly so: after all, on the night of January 1, 1994, just as the so-called North American Free Trade Agreement, NAFTA, among Canada, the United States, and Mexico, was about to go into effect, he stormed onto the stage.

Lightning and thunder followed.

It was a night to remember. As José Juárez, a Chiapas local, described it, "it was on New Year's Eve when President Carlos Salinas de Gortari retired to his chambers thinking he would wake up a North American. Instead he woke up a Guatemalan."

No, said the Subcomandante. Mexico isn't ready for the First World. Not yet.

Everywhere people rejoiced. *¡Un milagro!* A miracle! A wonder of wonders! So spoke Bishop Samuel Raúl Ruíz García, the bishop of San Cristóbal, whose role in the Zapatista revolution angered conservatives, but who was endorsed by millions worldwide, turning him into a favorite for the Nobel Peace Prize.

With his trademark black skintight mask, El Sup was constantly on television. *Un enmascarado:* Mexicans turned him into a god. Since pre-Columbian times Mexico has been enamored of the mask. A wall between the self and the universe, it serves as a shield and a hiding place. The mask is omnipresent in Mexico: in theaters, on the Day of the Dead, in *lucha libre,* the popular Latin American equivalent of wrestling. And among pop heroes like El Zorro, El Santo the wrestler, and Super Barrio, all defenders of *los miserables,* masked champions whose silent faces embody the faces of millions.

Suddenly, the guerrilla was back in fashion. The "news" that the Hispanic world had entered a new era of democratic transition had been proven wrong. Once again weapons, not ballots, were the order of the day. Within the year, the lost "motorcycle diary" of Ché Guevara was published in Europe and the United States—a record of a twenty-four-year-old Ché's travels on a Norton 500 from Argentina to Chile, Peru, Colombia, and Venezuela. A free-spirited, first-person account unlike any of his "mature" works, it recalled Sal Paradise's hitchhiking in Jack Kerouac's *On the Road.* El Sup had discovered new territory: the revolutionary as easy rider.

El Sup had a rifle, yes, but he hardly used it. His bullets took the form of faxes and e-mails, cluster bombs in the shape of communiqués and nonstop e-mail midrashim through the Internet. He wrote in a torrent, producing hundreds of texts, quickly disproving Hannah Arendt's claim that "under conditions of tyranny it is far easier to act than to think." In less than twelve months, during sleepless sessions on the word processor in the midst of fighting a war, El Sup generated enough text for a 300-

Zapatista action figures, San Cristóbal, Chiapas, Mexico, photo by Marirosa Toscani Ballo. Courtesy of *Colors.*

page volume. And he sent it out without concern for copyright. His goal was to subvert our conception of intellectual ownership, to make the private public and vice versa.

He was a master at marketing. By presenting himself as a down-to-earth dissenter, a nonconformist, a hipster dressed up as soldier, he made it easy to feel close to him. To fall in love with him, even. In one communiqué, for instance, he addresses the Mexican people:

> Brothers and sisters, we are the product of five hundred years of struggle: first against slavery; then in the insurgent-led war of Independence against Spain; later in the fight to avoid being absorbed by North American expansion; next to proclaim our Constitution and expel the French from our soil; and finally, after the dictatorship of Porfirio Díaz refused

to fairly apply the reform laws, in the rebellion where
the people created their own leaders. In that rebellion
Villa and Zapata emerged—poor men, like us.

In another, he writes to his fellow Zapatistas:

Our struggle is righteous and true; it is not a
response to personal interests, but to the will for
freedom of all the Mexican people and the indigenous
people in particular. We want justice and we will
carry on because hope also lives in our hearts.

And in a letter to President Clinton, El Sup ponders:

We wonder if the United States Congress and the
people of the United States of North America
approved this military and economic aid to fight the
drug traffic or to murder indigenous people in the
Mexican Southeast. Troops, planes, helicopters,
radar, communications technology, weapons and
military supplies are currently being used not to
pursue drug traffickers and the big kingpins of the
drug Mafia, but rather to repress the righteous
struggle of the people of Mexico and of the
indigenous people of Chiapas in the southeast of our
country, and to murder innocent men, women, and
children.
    We don't receive any aid from foreign
governments, people, or organizations. We have
nothing to do with national or international drug
trafficking or terrorism. We organized ourselves of
our own volition, because of our enormous needs and
problems. We are tired of so many years of deception
and death. It is our right to fight for a dignified life.
At all times we have abided by the international laws
of war and respected the civil population.

Since all the other compañeros of the Zapatista National Liberation
Army were more modest, El Sup stole the spotlight. He was unquestionably *la estrella*. And his enigmatic identity began to obsess people. His
education, some said, is obviously extensive. He must be a product of
the *Distrito Federal,* the Mexico City of the early eighties.

Was he overwhelmed by the outpouring of public affection? "I won't put much stock in it," he told one interviewer.

> I don't gain anything from it and we're not sure the organizations will, either. I guess I just don't know. About what's going on. I only get an inkling of what's going on when a journalist gets angry because I don't give him an interview. I say, "Since when am I so famous that they give me a hard time about being selective, and the lights, and I don't know what all." That is pure ideology, as they say up there, no? We don't have power struggles or ego problems of any kind.

Being selective: *el discriminador*. But his ego, no doubt, is monumental. He courted attention relentlessly. By 1995, stories circulated that internal struggles within the Zapatistas were growing, fought over El Sup's stardom.

Meanwhile, unmasking El Sup became a sport. Who is he? Where did he come from? I, for one, thought I knew, though not through any feat of journalistic prowess. I haven't been to the Chiapas jungle since the Zapatistas launched their rebellion. And if he is who I think he is, I haven't spoken to him since long before his communiqués began streaming from the Lacandonian rain forest.

The clue to his identity came in early 1995, after Salinas had ceded power to his successor, Ernesto Zedillo Ponce de León, in the aftermath of a series of political assassinations that had rocked the PRI, the governing party. The enemy grew restless. El Sup had become too dangerous. And too popular! He was better known than any politician. He commanded more attention than any of the soap operas on Mexican TV, the opiate of the Mexican masses. Enough was enough. It was time for him to go.

Desenmascarar. What the Mexican government performed was an ancient ritual at the heart of the nation's soul: the unmasking. Quetzalcoatl was unmasked by the Spaniards, Sor Juana by the Church, and Pancho Villa by a spy. To unmask can mean to undo, or to destroy, but it can also mean to elevate to a higher status: every six years, as the country prepares to receive its new president, the head of the PRI literally unveils his successor before everyone eyes.

In the public eye—El Sup's own terrain—Mexican government revealed his true self: Rafael Sebastián Guillén Vicente, a thirty-seven-year-old former college professor. A revelation, indeed, which El Sup immediately disputed . . . before vanishing into the night. Just like that, he disappeared. Off the TV screens. Out of the spotlight. He became a nonentity: *un espíritu*. Other Zapatistas replaced him in the high command of the Zapatista army.

In Mexico, of course, the government is always wrong; that is, since it promotes itself as the sole owner of the Truth, nobody believes it. And yet, El Sup might well be Guillén. I personally have no trouble equating the two. They sounded the same, right down to their rhetoric—a language I learned at the Xochimilco campus of Mexico City's Universidad Autónoma Metropolitana (UAM), the decidedly radical school where Guillén taught. In discussing his communiqués with several old college friends, we were struck by the similarities between his postmodern tongue and the often hallucinatory verbiage at Xochimilco, full of postscripts and qualifications and references to high and low, from modernist literature and academic Marxism to pop culture. El Sup said his idols were the nationally known "new journalists" Carlos Monsiváis and Elena Poniatowska, whom my whole intellectual generation deeply admired and whose own works trespass intellectual boundaries with glee. When asked to describe the books that influenced him, he would cite the seventies writing of Octavio Paz, Julio Cortázar, Mario Vargas Llosa, and Gabriel García Márquez, although he would be careful to distance himself from the right-wing politics of Paz and Vargas Llosa.

El Sup mooned journalists with his writings. His speeches, like the authors we studied at UAM, seamlessly mix fiction with reality, becoming masterful self-parodies, texts about texts about texts. In a reply to a letter from the University Student Council of the University Nacional Autónoma de México (UNAM), he writes that with great pleasure the Zapatistas have received the students' support. He asks them to get organized following the pattern of the Zapatistas, and concludes:

> If you accept this invitation, we need you to send
> some delegates so that, through an intermediary, we
> can arrange the details. We must organize everything
> well so that spies from the government don't slip
> through. And if you make it down, don't worry about

it. But keep up the fight over where you are, so that there can be justice for all Mexican people.

That's all, men and women, students of Mexico. We will be expecting a written response from you.

> Respectfully,
>
> From the mountains of the
> Mexican Southeast.

P.S.: El Sup's section: "The repeating post-script."

Another postscript follows, and then more and more.

> P.P.S.: As long as we're in the P.S.'s, which of all the "University Student Councils" wrote to us? Because back when I was a stylish young man of 25 . . . there were at least three of them. Did they merge?

> P.S. to the P.S. to the P.S.: In the event that you do (whew!) take the Zócalo, don't be selfish. . . . Save me some space where I can at least sell arts and crafts. I may have to choose between being an unemployed "violence professional" and an underemployed one, with underemployment wages (much more marketable that way, under NAFTA, you know).

> P.S. to the nth power: These postscripts are really a letter disguised as a postscript (to hide it from the Attorney General's Office and all the rest of the strongmen in dark glasses), and, but of course, it requires neither an answer, nor a sender, nor an addressee (an undeniable advantage of a letter disguised as a postscript).

> Nostalgic P.S.: When I was young (Hello, Attorney General's Office. Here comes more data), there used to be a lightly wooded place between the main library, the Facultad de Filosofa y Letras, the Torre de Humanidades, Insurgentes Avenue and the interior circuit of Ciudad Universitaria. We used to call that space, for reasons obvious to the initiates, the "Valley of Passions," and it was visited assiduously by diverse

elements of the fauna who populated at 7 P.M. (an
hour when those of good conscience drink hot
chocolate and the bad ones make themselves hot
enough to melt); they came from the humanities,
sciences, and other areas (are there others?). At that
time, a Cuban (Are you ready, Ambassador Jones?
Make a note: more proof of pro-Castro tendencies)
who used to give lectures seated in front of piano keys
the color of his skin . . . and who called himself
Snowball, would repeat over and over, "You can't
have a good conscience and a heart. . . ."

Final fortissimo P.S.: Have you noticed how
exquisitely cultured and refined these postscripts are?
Are they not worthy of the First World? Don't they
call attention to the fact that we "transgressors,"
thanks to NAFTA are striving to be competitive?

"Happy Ending" P.S.: Okay, okay, I'm going. This
trip is coming to an end, and the guard, as usual, is
still asleep and someone is tired of repeating "Is
anybody out there?" and tell myself, "Our country"
. . . and what is your answer?

El Sup's unconventional style was a commonplace at UAM in the early
eighties. I was a student there at the time, the same time that Guillén,
about five years my elder, was teaching. Some of my friends took classes
with him, remarking on his sharp intellect and infectious verbosity.
Crossing paths with him in hallways and cafeterias, I remember him as
bright and articulate.

Well-known as an incubator for Marxist, pro-Cuba, pro-Sandanista
activity, UAM's Xochimilco campus had been built by the government
in the early seventies. It included two other campuses in far-flung corners of the city. It was built in an attempt to dilute the massive student
population at UNAM, the oldest institution of higher learning in the
country.

In her book, *La noche de Tlatelolco,* Poniatowska chronicled the protests of 1968. It was UNAM's student body, some 30,000 strong, who led
the protests, which were brutally crushed in the massacre at Tlatelolco
Square. El Sup, although not Guillén, was born during that massacre—

a ritual birth, an origin in which his whole militant odyssey was prefigured. If the revolution couldn't be won in the nation's capital, he would join the unhappy peasants in Chiapas and Yucatán—he would become an urban exile.

When Xochimilco opened, it immediately superseded UNAM in antigovernment militancy. It became a magnet for subversive artists, would-be guerrilla fighters, and sharp-tongued political thinkers. The place was known for its unorthodox educational methods, and fields of study often lost their boundaries. Professors not only sensitized us to the nation's poverty and injustice, they encouraged us to take action. Friends would take time off to travel to distant rural regions and live with the indigenous people. Most eventually returned, but many didn't—they simply vanished, adopting new identities and new lives.

Injustice, inequality, freedom of speech—we wanted changes. "Down with the one-party system!" We would take advantage of cheap fares and travel to Havana, to become eyewitnesses to the profound transformation that had taken place in a corner of the Hispanic world. The Sandinistas in Nicaragua captured our attention and love. We admired their courage and identified with intellectuals like Julio Cortázar, Ernesto Cardenal, and Sergio Ramírez, who had put their literary careers on hold to work for the Nicaraguan government, or who had orchestrated international campaigns to support the Sandinista fight. We were excited— and we were blind. Our personal libraries were packed full with Marxist literature. Our writers were busy fashioning a style in which art and politics were inseparable. We disregarded any argument that tried to diminish our utopian expectations.

Indeed, finding bridges between political theory and activism became a sport. Those of us who studied psychology embraced the antipsychiatry movement and were expelled from asylums for allowing patients to go free. I, for one, worked with a metropolitan priest, Padre Chinchachoma, who devoted his ministry to homeless children. He believed that to help the children he needed to live among them, in Mexico City's garbage dumps—foraging with them for food, making and selling drugs for money, and occasionally engaging in acts of vandalism. I read Padre Chinchachoma's books with great admiration. He was my messiah, my Sup before El Sup.

Xochimilco—exciting, contradictory. Our teachers were dissatisfied middle-class Mexican leftists, exiled Argentinean intellectuals, and other Latin American émigrés. Our idols were Ché Guevara, Felix Guattari, Antonio Gramsci, and Herbert Marcuse. Wealthy professors urged us to agitate among peasants in the countryside. And, what's more, we were aware that the government perceived our radicalism, our animosity, as productive.

In fact, it wanted our hatred. Its rationale was clear: if adolescents in the Third World are always full of antigovernment feeling, they should be provided with a secluded space to vent their rage. They'll scream, they'll organize, but as long as they're kept in isolation, nothing will come of it. And so we did, investing our time and energy in countless hopeless insurrectionary projects. But it wasn't a waste of energy. Something great did come out of it: El Sup.

I left Mexico in 1985, but I often look back at my years at UAM as a turning point. Between the pen and the sword, I thought I was wise for choosing the pen. But El Sup was even wiser: he chose both.

My politics and artistic views have changed somewhat. I have become a critic and scholar and have adopted a new language. In the process, I acquired a new mask of my own: I became part Mexican and part North American—at once both and neither.

Evidently, El Sup is also an academic, although a less reticent one. I was the coward, the egotist. He was the hero. We are both bridges— across cultures, across social classes. I chose the library as my habitat, while he made Mexico itself his personal creation.

So what if he is Guillén, and vice versa? Simply that his unmasking has served its purpose: El Sup has faded away from public attention. His once-omnipresent visage now appears infrequently, if at all, a haggard reminder of the still miserable conditions in the South.

Now there's talk of him, El Sup, becoming a leftist candidate in national politics. But history has little room for heroes shifting gears, and even less for legends who undress themselves. Besides, no career is more discredited in Mexico than that of a politician. Better to vanish: only then will his trademark become truly indelible. Or better still: to become a novelist. After all, Latin America is depressing in its politics, but vivid in its imaginings. Viva El Sup, the intangible—a giant of the imagination.

[1996]

SAM SPADE, *OTRA VEZ*

Somewhere in the middle of *Some Clouds,* a confusing if en-chanting petite novel, Héctor Belascoarán Shayne, a damned private eye in the hard-boiled tradition of Raymond Chandler's Philip Marlowe, invites himself to his creator's house in Colonia Condesa, a central neigh-borhood in Mexico City. The metafictional device recalls the art of Miguel de Unamuno, Pirandello, and Felipe Alfau, in which a writer confronts his own literary characters to discuss the anxiety of modern civilization. But Paco Ignacio Taibo II, arguably Mexico's most popular novelist, is anything but a pompous postmodernist: His thirty-odd titles are natu-ralistic in style and critical of establishment politics, but never book-ishly sophisticated. He and Belascoarán, who doesn't believe in logical thinking, have a conversation in which they share jokes, confess past sins, and drink a few Cokes. At one point they discuss literature (Norman Mailer, John Dos Passos, Jim Thompson, Rodolfo Walsh), though not in arrogant, condescending fashion.

Once an engineer but now a self-employed advocate who rails against institutionalized corruption and shares a tiny office with a plumber, an upholsterer and a sewer-and-drainage expert, Belascoarán is Mexico's contemporary hero of the oppressed, a detective with a lot of mileage in exploring the innermost symbols of the collective national psyche. He has two exotic last names, says a segment of *Some Clouds,*

> and one eye less than most people. He was thirty-
> five years old, with an ex-wife, an ex-lover, one
> brother, one sister, a denim suit that made him look
> more like a social anthropologist than a detective, a
> .38 automatic in a drawer in his office in Mexico City,

a slight limp from an old bullet wound in his right leg,
and a private investigator's license he'd gotten
through a correspondence course. He had a marked
predilection for soft drinks, and certain Hemingway
novels (the first one and the next to the next to the
last). . . . He slept less than six hours a night, he liked
the soft sound ideas made when they came together
inside his head, and he'd spent the last five years
bearing up under the strange weight of an
inexplicable fatigue, awash in a sea of memories,
reliving wasted passions, idiot love affairs, old
routines that had once seemed exciting. He didn't
think too highly of himself in general, although he did
have a good deal of respect for his capacity for
bullheaded stubbornness.

Belascoarán is trying to solve the mysterious death of a millionaire's
heirs, and somebody told him that his creator (PITII, as he likes to be
known), although not a writer of Nobel Prize caliber, had sharpness
enough to sort out labyrinth clues. Their dialogue has amusing moments,
like the following, in which the novelist offers a portrait of himself and
Mexico. "This country will kill you," he says.

It'll kill you in a lot of different ways. It'll kill you
with corruption, out of boredom, out of meanness,
it'll kill you with hunger, unemployment, with cold,
with bullets, it'll beat you to death. . . . I've spent the
last thirteen years fighting the system. I was in the
student movement in '68, I was active for a while in
leftist politics, I worked with the unions, with factory
workers, organizing, putting out magazines,
pamphlets. I can't tell you how many good jobs I've
left behind. I've never been interested in just making
myself a bunch of money. I never worked for the PRI
[the ruling political party], I don't owe anything, or
almost nothing, when I fucked up I never got
anybody killed, and if I fucked somebody over it was
out of ineptitude and stupidity and not because I'd
sold out or was an asshole, no one ever paid me not to
do what I believed in, I worked at a lot of stupid jobs

> but I always did things the best that I knew how. . . . If
> I can write the truth and find someone to print it,
> that's OK.

Such a code of ethics and honesty, mixed with avant-garde narrative technique, is PITII's *lettre de créance*. Born in 1949 in Asturias, Spain, he is a prolific historian, journalist and writer who publishes at a rate of three titles a year, mostly in cheap editions fraught with typos but quickly devoured by the masses. His major theme is the past and present of his adoptive country, Mexico, where he has lived since childhood. He is comfortable describing the intellectual journey of the union leader Ricardo Flores Magón, the ideological struggle of muralists José Clemente Orozco and Diego Rivera, and the political apprenticeship of Ché Guevara and Fidel Castro. Because of his mass-market appeal (and perhaps partly his professed left-wing affiliations), until recently he was largely ignored by both private and state media, his books seldom reviewed in newspapers or on television.

Still, every new title of his becomes a huge best seller. Why? How to explain the phenomenon that also sweeps the novels of Guadalupe Loeza, Laura Esquivel, and others to the top of the sales charts? The answer— what PITII unabashedly calls a "reader's democracy"—has to do with Mexican pop culture, in PITII's case a fascination with the detective novel, his ticket to success.

In Latin America as a whole, this genre has had a beguiling life.* As an intellectual game, it was cultivated in the forties by Borges, his friend Adolfo Bioy Casares, and others in the River Plate. Some three decades later came a rebellion against middle-class values, speeded by popular unrest over dictatorial regimes and an admiration for the Beat generation, and a new wave of investigator was born, one identified with urban roughness and anarchy, with the unpolite mien of a Philip Marlowe. An investigator like Erik Lönnrot in Borges's story "Death and the Compass" gave way to fearless private eyes like Belascoarán, urban dwellers, and instinctual sociologists ready to embark on the study of their immediate environments. In Rio de Janeiro, Santiago de Chile and Mexico

---

* *See my book* Antiheroes: Mexico and Its Detective Novel, *translated by Jesse H. Lytle and Jennifer A. Mattson (Cranbury, N.J.: Fairleigh Dickinson University Press, 1997).*

City, among other venues, this unconventional hero, a guy with little patience and no interest in cerebral enterprises, became a rebuttal of orderly life and the status quo, a way to oppose the government, to protest U.S. military intervention and to increase social awareness.

Twice the winner of the Hammett International Prize, PITII is acknowledged as the principal promoter of this new style of detective fiction in the Southern Hemisphere. Always half-baked and chaotically structured, his novels have in fact injected a freshness into Latin American literature that had been flagging since the boom generation that includes Mario Vargas Llosa, Julio Cortázar, and Gabriel García Márquez—which isn't to say they are of equal stylistic quality. His themes range from sports to religion, from the 1910 Socialist Revolution to the oil refineries during the Lázaro Cárdenas regime. Indeed, many echo the topics discussed by Paz in *The Labyrinth of Solitude*: The unresolved mystery of a goalie from the Jalisco major-league soccer team is an excuse to analyze Mexico's passion for football; an investigation in a construction feud over the new Basílica of Guadalupe allows the writer to discuss the nation's Catholicism; and the rumor that Emiliano Zapata, assassinated in 1919 on the Chinameca Ranch, is still alive in a secret cave in the state of Morelos, offering spiritual support to armed guerrillas in Central and South America, is a juicy means to study the field of folk heroes. PITII's portrait of Mexico City as hell on earth, a labyrinth of pollution, vandalism, and moral promiscuity, a true habitat for unredeemed souls, is nothing but enchanting. No novelist since Fuentes, particularly in *Where the Air Is Clear,* has described the most populated metropolis on the globe with more power.

If anything, PITII will be remembered for creating Héctor Balascoarán Shayne, a character who is a voracious smoker of cheap Delicado filters, likes to take vacations in *lumpen* motels in Acapulco, is an admirer of Michael Strogoff, John Reed, and Zorro, loves the trova of Silvio Rodríguez, and has a good sense of humor. To such a degree has the protagonist become a part of Mexico's pop consciousness that when he was killed in one of the saga's installments (*Return to the Same City,* 1989), PITII found himself in a plight similar to Conan Doyle's when he got tired of Sherlock Holmes and decided to end it all. He was bombarded with petitions from readers to revive the detective. So, Belascoarán came back to life, the next time out recovering from a wound that was nearly fatal.

Those unacquainted with PITII's work should start with the novel under review. Originally written in 1984 and the fourth to be translated into English (the others, chronologically, are *An Easy Thing, The Shadow of the Shadow,* and *Calling All Heroes*), it offers an ample display of the writer's pathos and obsessions and also a sideboard of his shortcomings. As always, the plot, a bit loose and nonsensical, is an excuse to display a wide range of antigovernment, though not particularly partisan, opinions and to build a portrait of Mexico City as a bizarre and chaotic milieu. Detailing the slow disintegration of an aristocratic family with millions in stocks, international bank accounts, and real estate, Belascoarán is asked to protect Anita, the sole inheritor of the fortune, and to determine the identity of the one attempting to steal her money.

A couple of subplots are intertwined, with the archenemy, Arturo Melgar (nicknamed "The Rat," a sickly anti-Communist gangster on the payroll of the PRI but also the detective's onetime schoolmate), acquiring near mythic stature as villain. In the end, *Some Clouds* is no paean to justice and morality—an unlikely message in a country like Mexico, whose road to modernity has never been free from suffering and confusion. On the contrary, PITII turns the genre upside down by allowing disorder and abuse to prevail. The reader's basic enjoyment comes from a rendezvous, through baroque and carnivalesque byways, with Mexico's soul.

With a reputation now as being something of a one-man literary guerrilla, the place of PITII in the Mexican intelligentsia might soon change from outspoken critic to mainstream voice. Popular appeal cannot keep him in the margins for much longer. But even if recognition by the establishment transforms him from *enfant terrible* to convenient dissenter, his history as a sort of literary Robin Hood who both pleases and infuriates has already made its mark. His nearly unbalanced yet engaging oeuvre is required reading for followers of the tradition of hard-boiled private eyes—and also for those who are not but find themselves intrigued by popular culture south of the border.

[1992]

Miguel Covarrubias, *Cantinflas,* 1937. Reproduced courtesy of the Cineteca Nacional, Mexico City.

THE RIDDLE OF CANTINFLAS

In everything that can be called art there is a quality of redemption.

Raymond Chandler

Culture in Mexico is governed by two opposing sides, sharply divided by an open wound: on the one hand, a high-brow, European-ized elite dreams of inserting the nation's creative talent into a global stream of artistic consciousness; on the other, native art, a hybrid that results from ancient and borrowed elements, is produced by and for the masses. High-brow: Frida Kahlo; the painters Rufino Tamayo, José Clemente Orozco, Diego Rivera, and David Alfaro Siqueiros; the globe-trotting opera singer Plácido Domingo; even the Russian and Spanish filmmakers Sergei Einsenstein (*¡Que viva México!*) and Luis Buñuel (*Los olvidados*), who greatly influenced the nation's self-understanding through powerful cinematic images. Low-brow: the popular wrestler El Santo; the *ranchera* movies of the thirties and forties with Pedro Infante, Jorge Negrete, Blanca Estela Pavón, and Lupe Vélez; the arch famous children's songwriter Francisco Gabilondo Soler, *aka* Cri-Cri; and the romantic balladist Juan Gabriel. Don't worry if you're unable to recognize the latter references: the nation's cultural exports are invariably Westernized products, hardly any proletarian items.

A common belief has it that low-brow Mexican culture is kitschy. Nothing is further from the truth. The terms *kitsch* and *camp*, which *Webster's Dictionary* defines as "artwork characterized by sentimental, often pretentious bad taste" and "something so outrageously artificial, affected, inappropriate, or out-of date to be considered amusing," don't even have an equivalent in Spanish; *cursi*, meaning parodic, self-referential, inbred with intentional exaggeration, or perhaps misrepresentation, of human feelings, is the closest in esthetic terminology Spanish gets to them. But American icons like the Lawrence Welk Show, Barry Manilow, and the Bee Gees are *cursi*; native art in Mexico, instead, is nothing but *rascuache,* a south-of-the-border colloquialism ignored by the Iberian standardizer, the *Diccionario de la Real Academia Española,* yet often used in Mexico to describe a cultural item of inferior quality and proletarian origin.

Rascuache has no English cognate: the Pachuco fashion style in Los Angeles, for example, is *rascuache*; the musician Agustín Lara; the porcelain replicas of smiling clowns and ballerinas known as Lladrós, sold at department stores; imitations of Yves St. Laurent and Ralph Lauren clothing; t-shirts of the music group Menudo; native soda such as Chaparritas and flavored Tehuacán; tamarind and coconut candy; in spite of their global recognition (or perhaps as a result of it), the novelists Laura Esquivel, responsible for *Like Water for Chocolate,* and Paco Ignacio Taibo II, known for dirty-realist thrillers that have Private Detective Héctor Belascoarán Shayne as protagonist, are somewhat *rascuache* as well. While Mexico's high-brow society uses and abuses the term in order to establish a distance, to distinguish itself from cheap, low-born inventiveness, *rascuachismo,* with its trademark of authenticity, is also a source of pride and self-respect among the dispossessed. It is applied by the bourgeoisie to *alguien más*—someone else judged to be outside the demarcations of approved taste and decorum: to be *rascuache* is to be inferior, undeserving. But the lower classes assume its esthetics with a happy smile: a *rascuache* item is truly, unequivocally Mexican and therefore a magnet of self-satisfaction. Throughout the decades, *rascuachismo* has acquired something like a logic of taste, a consistent sensibility which can be crammed into the mold of a system. Avant-garde bourgeois art, even when addressing the most vulgar and tasteless, will by definition never descend to such low esteem. But the ruling class always maintains a kind of "negotiating relationship" with it; it uses it to establish a bridge across economic and social lines, to create an image of the nation's collective psyche, and to benefit the tourist industry.

As proven by the case of the early twentieth-century engraver José Guadalupe Posada, occasionally a proletarian artist can be "saved" from his *rascuache* background through the help of enlightened, upper-class artists. Posada died poor and forgotten and was buried in an anonymous grave in 1913, as the Socialist Revolution was sweeping the country. His lampoons ridiculed Porfirio Díaz's dictatorship (1876–1911) and commemorated holidays and natural disasters. But he would have remained anonymous had Jean Charlot, a French immigrant to Mexico and a friend of muralists Rivera and Orozco, not shown Posada's prints around and written about him in the context of the European style, Cubism. He brought him to international attention, thus redeeming him from the imprisonment of *rascuachismo* and turned him into a veritable artifact of high-brow culture. In other cases, nonetheless, a *rascuache* artist will be used by the intelligentsia to promote a certain "official" vision of the country, only to be dropped when such vision becomes either unnecessary or obstructive. Popular arts and crafts endure and grow because they fulfill certain functions within nationalism and capitalist reproduction, and because they offer a valuable mirror through which to sell an accepted, convenient image of society as a whole. For example, the anthropologist Néstor García Canclini, author of *Transforming Modernity: Popular Culture in Mexico,* has written eloquently on the values of *rascuache* art, folklore, and aboriginal souvenirs for a certain government regime interested in sponsoring the production of export artifacts among the lower classes for purely touristy purposes. They sell and they offer an image of Mexico as intimately connected with its pre-Colombian roots: a nation with a historic past and a non-Western philosophy of life, a civilization thirty splendorous centuries in the making.

The art critic Tomás Ybarra-Frausto, in a stimulating 1990 essay, explains in more detail this attractive concept, *rascuachismo:*

> Propriety and keeping up appearances—*el qué dirán*—are the codes shattered by the attitude of *rascuachismo*. This outsider viewpoint stems from a funky, irreverent stance that debunks convention and spoofs protocol. To be *rascuache* is to posit a bawdy, spunky consciousness, to seek to subvert and turn ruling paradigms upside down. It is a witty, irreverent, and impertinent posture that recodes and moves outside established boundaries.

While pertaining to Mexican culture in general, Ybarra-Frausto's study is centered on the Chicano community of the Southwest, where, to distinguish itself from its Mexican past, it becomes something of an insider's private code. "Very generally," he argues, "*rascuachismo* is an underdog perspective—a view from *los de abajo,* an attitude rooted in resourcefulness and adaptability, yet mindful of stance and style. . . . It presupposes the worldview of the have-nots, but is also a quality exemplified in objects and places (a *rascuache* car or restaurant) and in social comportment (a person who is or acts *rascuache*)." Ybarra-Frausto suggests a random list of *rascuache* items akin to the Mexican-American community: the Royal Chicano Air Force, paintings on velvet, the calaveras of Posada, and the movie by Cheech Marín, *Born in East L.A.* He then distinguishes levels of *medio* and *muy,* low and high *rascuachismo*: Microwave tamales, the comedian Tin Tán, shopping at K-Mart, flour tortillas made with vegetable oil, pretending you are Spanish, and portraits of Emiliano Zapata on velvet slippers (*chanclas*) belong to the first category; to the second, frozen capirotada, flour tortillas made with lard, being bilingual and speaking with an accent in both languages, shopping at J. C. Penney's, portraits of Francisco Villa on velvet *chanclas,* and Cantinflas. Which brings me back to kitsch and camp, two terms implying a sense of parody and self-consciousness never found in *rascuachismo.* A *rascuache* artifact will not become emblematic of low-brow Mexicanness until the sophisticated elite, always an alien force, says so— that is, until it is rescued to become a souvenir, a Mexican curiosity in the universal archives of Western civilization.*

Of the whole *rascuache* galaxy in Mexican low-brow culture, Cantinflas, Ybarra-Frausto's last entry, is of particular interest to me. In spite of his incredibly high profile south of the border, today he is virtually unknown in Europe and the United States, which, I am sure, is directly related to the lack of sympathy with which the Mexican sophisticated elite views him nowadays. Indeed, this most revered Spanish-speaking comedian, admired at first by the middle class and the ruling intelligentsia, aside from the masses, of course, illustrates the never-ending rivalries between high and low culture, between elitist and *rascuache* perspectives in Mexico and the Hispanic hemisphere at large.

---

* *I explore the issue of* rascuachismo *and Chicano politics in* Bandido *(New York: HarperCollins, 1995).*

His fame and decline show what's hot and cold, in and out, south of the border—and why.

Cantinflas, whose real name was Fortino Mario Alonso Moreno Reyes, was the *peladito* par excellence—a lumpen, street-wise itinerant citizen, the master of *mal gusto*—bad taste. He's slightly abusive, often disoriented, never totally happy, in total control of *la peladez,* with an irreverence that at once highlights and eases the tension between upper and lower classes in Mexico. Cantinflas's *rascuachismo* is also Mexico's. When he first appeared on stage, in the late thirties, the sophisticated elite championed him as a crystalline expression of the native soil. But by the time he died, at the age of eighty-one, he had become a casualty in the struggle to find an identity that suited the ruling party's desire to be part of the industrialized world. His mannerisms, his simplicity, while still adored by the populace, are today largely ignored by high-brow Mexican culture. Obviously, a drastic change of heart had taken place in the nation's mood.

A symptom of such a change is the fact that, when Cantinflas passed away, on April 20, 1993, he never received an obituary in *Vuelta,* Octavio Paz's literary monthly, probably the best cultural thermometer south of the border by which one can understand the ups and downs of the Latin American literati. The magazine is a sideboard of cosmopolitanism and finesse, a catalogue of bourgeois taste, a promoter of Europeanized ways of thought and conduct. Everybody's favorite rascal, Cantinflas, on the other hand, symbolizes the rough-and-tumble slapdash in poor barrios, the treacherousness of the illiterate, the vitality of the dispossessed, the obscenity of working-class people. By the mid-nineties his appeal had certainly passed, at least for the ruling class. Determined to sell NAFTA, the North American Free Trade Agreement, to Canada and the United States, the Partido Revolucionario Institucional, PRI, led by President Carlos Salinas de Gortari, was interested in selling an altogether different image of Mexico, not as a perfidious and disloyal neighbor but as honest, stable, trustworthy, a country made by a growing, money-oriented middle-class hypnotized by the American Dream.

Cantinflas: an unpleasant face to be hidden. Cantinflas: an arbiter of low taste in the process of eradication. But he was viewed this way only among the wealthy and socially mobile because half a century after the splash he made as the ultimate master of *rascuachismo,* among the poor and dispossessed he still typifies, as least for the masses, Mexico's true heart and soul. It's the ruling class and the intelligentsia that have changed: first love, then rejection. The transformation is not surprising. Others have suffered a similar fate. Cantinflas's early achievements were rapidly capitalized by a segment of the Europeanized Mexican intelligentsia that saw him as the champion of the forfeited, a magnetic representative of the underdogs with a larger-than-life charisma. In 1948, for instance, Tamayo painted his portrait, *Retrato de Cantinflas,* and three years later, Rivera placed him at the center of his 1951 mural in Teatro de los Insurgentes, in Mexico's capital. But around 1968, when the regime of President Gustavo Días Ordaz ordered a massacre of students in Tlatelolco Square, just as the Olympic Games were about to take place, the country underwent a deep identity crisis. Good-bye to the disoriented *peladito.* No more disjointed, disheveled heroes. It was obvious that the PRI was starting to implement a less *rascuache,* more modernized image of Mexico. The nation was ready to abandon the Third World, to cease looking south to Latin America and begin looking north: to emulate Uncle Sam. The transformation would take place over a period of decades, and, in the end, Cantinflas and other similar lowlife symbols would become a mishap.

As a result of this increasingly incurable allergy to *rascuachismo* and pop art, the intellectual elite has generated almost no bibliography about Cantinflas, neither panoramic nor reflective. The index of Carlos Fuentes's *The Buried Mirror: Reflections on Spain and the New World,* makes no mention of his incomparable contribution to Hispanic humor. Here and there, some marginal references to him are made by others. The poet Salvador Novo, for instance, described his intrepid ascendance in *Nuevas grandeza mexicana*; the playwright Xavier Villaurrutia praised him in the magazine *Hoy*; and Jorge Ibargüengoitia, the comic novelist responsible for *The Dead Girls,* does refer to him in passing in an essay included in his 1991 collection, *Autopsias rápidas.* Perhaps the only serious, thought-provoking interest in Cantinflas can be found in Carlos Monsiváis, a practitioner of New Journalism *a la mexicana* attracted to the cultural manifestations of the underclass. A text of 1988 states: "The smiles and laughter that Cantinflas's performance still generates among Mexican and Latin American audiences are not incidental. . . . What is being applauded? His incoherence is the incoherence of the masses, the aggression that is ignorance among the ruling class, the memorizing joke that is certified to be repeated, time and again, with success." And Monsiváis adds:

> Cantinflas, programmatic mumbling and conditioned reflex. He shows up, he moves, he begins a verbal twist, he puzzles his listener, he makes fun of the knowledge never captured in linguistic chaos . . . and his audience is bamboozled, is entertained and feels happy, finds inspiration in everyone's joy. . . . Cantinflas is a true Son of the People, the idiosyncratic expression that will become our tradition. This powerful asset allows the comedian-impresario to overcome the numerous mistakes of his films and generate permanent admiration through the gag in which there's much talk but nothing is said. What's humorous in Cantinflas: his image and voice; his comic message; his silhouette. The myth, a function of memory.

The only available biography of Cantinflas is a second-rate, "official" one written in 1994 by Guadalupe Elizalde: *Mario Moreno y Cantinflas . . . rompen el silencio.* Full of innuendoes, repetition, unverified information, typos, and spelling mistakes, its quality encapsulates the comedian's *rascuache* spirit: it confuses and deceives. It details the tense relationship he had with Mario Arturo Moreno, his illegitimate son, and the scandalous suicide of one of Moreno Reyes's lovers, the United States model Marion Roberts. But the biography does succeed in delivering an image of him as an institution: photographs of Cantinflas alongside every single Mexican president, from Días Ordaz to Miguel de la Madrid Hurtado, as well as with Lyndon Johnson and Richard Nixon, invade the volume. It discusses also his liaison with Mexico's Actor's Union, ANDA, which once accused him of mishandling the organization's money and of abusing his fame during a benefit performance for the Red Cross by embezzling donated funds.

But if studies about his life and oeuvre are almost nonexistent, his influence in Hispanic art is far-reaching. His name is invoked everyday on TV, the radio, and in the printed media. His movies are shown everywhere from Ciudad Juárez to Buenos Aires. Performance artists invoke his ghost. Musicians sing to his legend. Take the case of Luis Valdez, the legendary Chicano playwright and funding director of El Teatro Campesino in California and responsible for *Zoot Suit, La Bamba,* and other works. His 1973 epic play *La carpa de los Rascuachis* follows a Cantinflas-like protagonist from his crossing the border into the United States to the subsequent indignities he undergoes. Even if the name Cantinflas is never mentioned, the play is a direct homage, a tribute to this most durable and beloved comedian.

Lewis Jacobs once said of Charlie Chaplin that his importance lay not in what he contributed to film art, but in what he contributed to humanity. Cantinflas had a less universal, if equally ambitious impact: he remains an archetype, a model, a bottomless well of inspiration personifying the plight suffered by a preindustrial Mexico struggling to insert itself in the twentieth century. His adventures allow his audience to understand the transition from a rural to an urban setting many poor, uneducated campesinos have been forced to make in Latin America to earn only a few pesos. This means that, in spite of his cultural eclipse among the powerful, Cantinflas is an invaluable map to his nation's psyche, a compass to a *rascuache* esthetic, an invaluable tool to understand the clash between haves and have-nots in his society and culture. Through him we see, hear, and feel the Mexican self better. Posterity refuses to incorporate Moreno Reyes's villainous aspect; it prefers to remember him in an undiscriminating, uninformed, uncritical way—as the one and only *peladito.*

Born on August 12, 1911, in Santa María la Redonda, a poor neighborhood in Mexico City, Moreno Reyes was the son of a mailman, the sixth of thirteen children. A born entertainer, he charmed passers-by with his dancing and rapid-fire jokes and wordplay. As a teenager, he became, by turns, a bullfighter, a shoe-shine boy, a taxi driver, and a successful boxer before joining up with a *carpa,* an itinerant side show that combined circus acrobatics with slapstick comedy from the turn of the century to the advent of mass media in the forties. The *carpa* was a favorite gathering point for the disenfranchised mired in elemental daily struggle. A mixture of clowns, acrobats, and standup comedians, the *carperos* contributed a unique sense of *weltanshauung* to low-brow culture south of the border: they emphasized rapid corporeal movements interlaced with slapstick action, pratfalls, and verbal virtuosity. Tin Tán, Clavillazo, Mantequilla, and Resortes were all acclaimed comedians in the forties and fifties with a large following. Tin Tán in particular offered a different picture of *lo mexicano*. As John King, the British film and literary critic, argues in his book *Magical Reels*, "his Mexican-American pachuco, the zoot-suited, upwardly mobile con man, could talk and dance his way out of any difficult situation in a mixture of Spanglish idioms and border-music rhythms."

> The *pachuco* image had to be modified to suit the popular taste of the time, but the origins of Tin Tán—the border towns such as Ciudad Juárez, the mass migrations (legal and illegal) across the border, the Americanization of Mexican culture—were all to become an irresistible part of the Mexican experience. In *El rey del barrio* (King of the Neighborhood, 1949), his most memorable film, the verbal patter is exhilarating as are the spectacular dance situations with Tongolele (Yolanda Montes).

One night, the story goes, Cantinflas had to stand in for a sick master of ceremonies and made the audience laugh without end. The first thing he did was pee in his pants. Afterwards, nervous, virtually out of control, he became incoherent, his sentences tangling one another up, ridiculous. Instead of getting him boosted off the stage, his muddled patter was greeted with applause. Accident became routine. But the name Cantinflas only came into being when someone in the audience shouted (*En la cantina tú inflas!* (You tank up in the cantina! You're drunk!). The words conflated in Moreno Reyes's mind into a name: Cantinflas. It became his nom de guerre and ultimately entered the *Diccionario de la Real Academia Española* as a verb, *cantinflear,* which means to blather on and on and say nothing: as a noun, *cantinflada,* something done by an adorable clown; and as an adjective, *cantinfleando,* which means dumb. The combination produces the following dog-Latin expression: *Cantinflas cantinflea cantinfladas,* or Cantinflas blathers cantinflanisms.

Cantinfladas are heard everywhere in Mexico. The ear grows so accustomed to them, it quickly ceases to pay attention. An example of an eponymous one is the famous joke about one of Mexico's former presidents, Luis Echeverría Alvarez. In a legendary speech detailing the ruling party's political ideology, he is said to have explained: *No somos de la izquierda, ni de la derecha, sino todo lo contrario*—We are neither of the left, nor of the right, but entirely the opposite.

Cantinflas began as a supporting actor in 1937 and then married Valentina Zubareff (she died in 1966), the daughter of the owner of the *carpa* where he worked. It was she who suggested that Cantinflas appear in advertisements for products made in Mexico. The commercials were a success, so Moreno Reyes decided to found a film company, Posa Films, whose exclusive product would be movies starring Cantinflas. By 1941, the company had a couple of major Latin American hits, and Mario Moreno Reyes was well on his way to becoming a legend. During World War II, he met Miguel M. Delgado, who directed him in one hit after another, films such as the parodies *Romeo y Julieta* (1943) and *Gran Hotel* (1944). During those years, Moreno Reyes shaped the identity of his alter ego. Eventually, his creation would be recognized by visual and spiritual features a dirty, long-sleeve T-shirt; a rotten tie; baggy, patched pants always covering only half his buttock; a robe used as a belt; old, broken shoes; on his head a hat several sizes small; a sparse mustache and short, uncombed hair. He is the Spanish Golden Age's *pícaro* reincarnated: a scoundrel, a knave. When Cantinflas walks, he seems to be loose in his posture. When Cantinflas talks, he takes his hat off, switches it from one hand to another, and often hits the furniture or a friend with it to accentuate his anger or discomfort. Social mobility is taboo in Mexican society: once indigent, always underprivileged. Since classes are dogmatically rigid and unchangeable, Cantinflas ridicules the abysss between social groups and allows for relaxation and acceptance. He often goes from oppressed to oppressor, but no explosive conclusion is drawn. His movies lack an ideologically charged message inviting the unhappy to rebel. They open a space in which discomfort and complaint are dealt with through healthy laughter. This explains why the Mexican government endorsed Cantinflas when his image was useful: he makes the agitated masses happy; his subversive spirit works on the abstract, never upsetting the status quo. As Jonathan Kandell, a *New York Times* reporter, argues, Cantinflas "was riotously effective at deflating the rich and pompous, the staid and convention. . . . [He transformed the] apprehension of the burgeoning urban poor into laughter."

Mexicans constantly use verbal puzzles that demonstrate the cleverness of the speaker and challenge the wit of the audience. They are akin to *adivinanzas* and *rompecabezas,* riddles and brain-teasers, often obscene, as well as proverbs, unexpected rhymes, humorous naming, folk poetry, and shrewd puns. Through humor the nation handles collective and individual catastrophes and shortcomings. Only a few days after Pancho Villa was assassinated, in Hidalgo del Parral, in 1923, thousands of riddles and jokes circulated among the population. The same thing happened following the tragic 1985 earthquake in Mexico City. Whenever a group of Mexicans gets together at a friendly gathering, they invariably spend ten, fifteen minutes, perhaps longer, cracking jokes about politicians and television stars, food and habits. Such jokes have a linguistic edge personified by Cantinflas. A scene in the film *Ni sangre ni arena* (Neither Blood Nor Sand, 1941) exemplifies his linguistic bravado, his verbal virtuosity, and the often insurmountable difficulty in making him available through translation. Cantinflas is selling cigars—in Spanish *puros,* a word also meaning "only" and "pure"—outside a bullfighting arena. "Puros! Puros!," he says. Confusion takes place and he ends up selling tacos as well. "Puros! Tacos! Tacos! Puros!" More confusion takes place and Cantinflas is left without cigars, only with tacos. The humorous sequence concludes as he shouts: "Puros tacos! Tacos! Tacos puros!" Both *tacos* and *puros* have the same shape, except that the former is a symbol of Mexico's lower class, whereas the latter exemplifies the high-brow European aristocracy. By mixing them up, the comedian offers a sample of his world-view: social extremes south of the Rio Grande are based on cultural paraphernalia that, when scrambled, loses its power and invites laughter. Replace a rich white man's cigar with a taco and you get an average *mestizo.*

What is remarkable is the fashion in which Cantinflas's *rascuachismo* brought world literature to Mexico: his films adapted, or subverted, Shakespeare's *Romeo and Juliet,* Cervantes's *Don Quixote,* and Alexander Dumas's *The Three Musketeers.* As in vaudeville art, a single theme recurs in all of Cantinflas's films (available on VHS from Arkansas Entertainment, without subtitles): the mistaken identity. He is often confused with somebody else: a rich entrepreneur, a hotel bellboy, a corrupt policeman, Don Quixote. Plots circle around comic misunderstanding that allows for linguistic irreverence and pyrotechnics. One enters his universe without esthetic pretension and invariably leaves it with a sense of fulfillment: we have attended an enlightening rendezvous through the twisted behavioral paths of underprivileged Mexicans. He is the ultimate satirist, making fun of the macho husband, the virginal female, the abusive priest, the naive foreigner; but he also promotes the image of Mexicans as lazy, siesta-driven, immoral, and treacherous. By doing it, does he somehow perform a disservice to his people by poking fun at Hispanic mannerisms? He brings forth a sense of relaxation that allows for Mexican culture to cope with its tragedies and digest its shortcomings. Therefore, he proves (if proof was ever needed) that humor, while universal, is indistinctly local: there is nothing more difficult than translating it from one language to another, from one *entourage* to the next. Whenever Cantinflas ignites a hearty laughter, it's usually about something nonnatives would find unappealing, even insensitive. His oral jokes need to be explained, redesigned, and reformulated for foreigners to understand.

From 1939, when his first fifteen-minute-long films, *Siempre listo en las tinieblas* (Always Ready in Darkness) and *Jenjibre contra dinamita* (Ginger against Dynamite), were distributed, to 1981, when *El barrendero* (The Garbage Man), his last movie, was produced, he was the protagonist of a total of forty-seven films. Every single one was a huge box-office success, turning him into a millionaire. His comic talents were appreciated worldwide. Chaplin, for instance, is reported to have said, after watching a Cantinflas movie: "He's the greatest comedian alive . . . far greater than I am!" In Mexico and elsewhere in Hispanic America he was repeatedly the subject of innumerable homages and retrospectives and inspired a celebrated comic strip, many TV cartoons, and a weekly magazine called *Ahí está el detalle.* He was sought by diplomats and artists alike and was the symbol for the 1986 Soccer World Cup. Furthermore, rumors have it that since World War II, nobody else has been the runaway winner in every national presidential election, simply because the electorate knows its vote is ultimately irrelevant in a system plagued by fraud. Thus, Cantinflas becomes a much-beloved *subversivo* through which the population manifests its unhappiness with the undemocratic, repressive spirit it inhabits. A magnetic insurgent figure, Cantinflas is a proud ignoramus and a master in the lack of refinement. Ignorance is his weapon. He hides his illiteracy, stupidity, and lack of knowledge about

Dolores Camarillo "Fraustita" and Cantinflas, from *Ahí está el detalle*, directed by Juan Bustillo Oro, 1940. Archivo del Instituto Mexicano de Cinematografía. Reproduced courtesy of the Cineteca Nacional, Mexico City.

the importance of science and technology in the modern world by pretending he is a consummate master in just about everything, from quantum mechanics to Shakespeare. In that respect, he symbolizes twentieth-century Mexico's unfulfilled desire to be a contemporary of the rest of humankind.

His authentic talents, visual and verbal, cinematic and linguistic, are also the areas in which his country's art has reached higher distinction: pictorial art and literature. While in politics Mexico has always been unimaginative, the artistic legacy, from the Aztecs to Octavio Paz's 1990 Nobel Prize, is unquestionable. When attempting to find an equivalent in the English-speaking world, the obvious choice might appear to be Charlie Chaplin's wistful Little Tramp. Both use pantomime; both poke

Poster of *Ahí está el detalle.* Archivo del Instituto Mexicano de Cinematografía. Reproduced courtesy of the Cineteca Nacional, Mexico City.

fun at social types; both are unredeemed romantics, championing love as the true medicine of the human spirit; both refuse to approach film as a malleable, experimental art. But the similarities between the two are only superficial. Chaplin's creation was essentially a hostile character. His was a socially conscious message, inserted in the tradition of Jewish European liberalism, and his left-wing views often placed him at the center of heated controversies. In the era of silent cinema, which he refused to let go even when talkies were already dominating the market, his career achieved its apex from the twenties to the forties, in films such as *The Gold Rush, Modern Times,* and *The Great Dictator.* Cantinflas's main strength is in speech—his tongue is his main weapon. He twists and turns it; he talks nonsense ad infinitum to confuse and disorient. As critic Rosa Linda Fregoso claims in her 1993 study *The Bronze Screen,* he emerged as the unchallenged master of *cábula,* using "the subversive (and pleasurable) play with language . . . [he] satirized a rhetorical tendency of Mexican politicians known as *pura palabrería,* the excessive usage of words that said either 'nothing' or very little." He filled the vacuum of his solitude with verbs and adjectives, if only not to feel lonely and alone. While Chaplin's switch to talkies was challenging and ultimately unsuccessful, his mute hero, because of his unspecified background, achieved universality. Cantinflas, on the other hand, spent his energy exploring the intricacies of the Mexican collective self. Consequently, his art was overwhelmingly regional and parochial, and only through that particularity he achieved universality. Cantinflas's true Hollywood equivalents might be the Three Stooges, with their humorous vaudevillian sketches that captivated their audience in the late thirties; or, even better, the Marx Brothers. Their debut took place in 1929, and as Guadalupe Elizalde claims, in spite of his miserable English, Cantinflas was their loyal fan. Groucho's humor is based on funny looks and a caustic sense of laughter that uses ridiculous statements to philosophize about politics and daily life. W. C. Fields used to call the Marx Brothers "the only act I could not follow," and many Spanish-speakers often say the same about Cantinflas. While he uses (and abuses) sighs, shrugs, and grimaces, language is his strength—his aggressive weapon, his defense mechanism, his true forte, the crucial expression of his convoluted self. He conjugates verbs erroneously, invents adjectives and adverbs, and consistently fails to complete his sentences. In short, he reinvents the Spanish language, makes an idiosyncratic hybrid, a Mexican jargon, a *rascuache* code. Indeed, his verbal pyrotechnia is at its best when Cantinflas talks to the educated: he takes detours, repeats sentences, gets lost, starts all over again, The message is clear: in Mexico, high- and low-brow cultures live misunderstanding each other; they misrepresent, misquote, deceive, distort, and slant each other. The following transcription, representative of his convoluted style, comes from an interview published in the newspaper *Excélsior* on October 20, 1938:

> Vamos por partes: ¿Usted me pregunta que cuál ha
> sido mi mejor interpretación? ¿Y yo le tengo que
> responder que . . . ? ¿Qué le tengo que responder? ¿O
> usted me responde? Bueno, pero ¿qué relajo es éste? A
> ver, otra vez: usted quiere que le diga cuál ha sido, es
> y será, a través del devenir histórico-materialista-
> dialéctico, la mejor de mis interpretaciones
> proletarias. Y yo creo que hasta cierto punto, y si no,
> de todos modos, porque usted sabe que, al cabo y
> que, y como quiera que, la mejor de todas mis
> interpretaciones ha sido la interpretación racional y
> exacta del Universo conforme al artículo tercero. . . .
> ¿Qué? ¿Eso no . . . ? ¿Bueno, pues usted de qué habla?

An inevitably raw, insufficient translation. The reader should known that in Spanish, *interpretación* means simultaneously "performance" and "interpretation":

> Let's see: You're asking me which has been my best
> interpretations [e.g. performance]? And I have to
> answer that . . . ? What do I have to answer? Or is it
> you who should answer? OK, but what mess is this?
> Again, let's see: you want me to tell you which has
> been, is and will be, throughout historical-
> materialistic-dialectical, the best of my proletarian
> interpretations. And I believe that up to a certain
> point, and if not, in any case, because as you know,
> notwithstanding, and in spite of all, the best of my
> interpretations has been the rational and exact
> interpretation of the Universe, according to article 3.
> . . . What? It isn't true . . . ? OK, so what are you
> talking about?

Not long ago, during a one-day tribute at Lincoln Center's Walter Reade Theater, I had *Ahí está el detalle* (That's the Deal), his most famous movie, shown as part of a retrospective on modern Mexican cinema. The response was intriguing. Whereas the rest of the films, a product of contemporary artists, attracted a cosmopolitan, intellectually sophis-ticated audience, Cantinflas brought a large number of lower-class *hispanos* anxious to recapture a certain sight, a charming laughter of a native culture left behind. It was impossible to get a subtitled copy, which forced us to use simultaneous translation. Richard Peña, the Harvard-educated executive director of the New York Film Festival and a native Spanish-speaker of Puerto Rican background, took upon himself the impossible task of translating the comedian. Seeing him after the show was saddening: he was empty of all energy, humorless, completely mute. To understand his plight, imagine for a minute, doing a simultaneous translation of Woody Allen into Hebrew or German while retaining its New York sense of Jewish comedy.

In the forties the Mexican film industry underwent a tremendous transformation. From small studio productions to blockbusters, movies were delivered at an amazing speed and had a successful running throughout Hispanic America. Jorge Negrete, María Félix, Dolores del Río, and Pedro Infante populated the screen with peasant heroes, igno-rant and naive in the ways of the industrial world. As John King puts it: "The success of Mexican cinema in the forties was due to a series of circumstances: the added commercial opportunities offered by the war, the emergence of a number of important directors and cinematogra-phers and the consolidation of a star system resting on proven formu-lae." Cantinflas, in spite of his *rascuachismo*, worked with internationally renowned figures in Mexico: the Russian émigré Acady Boytler, a pupil of the theater director Konstantin Stanislawsky; the musician Silvestre Revueltas; the filmmaker Chano Urueta; the screenwriters Salvador Novo and Pepe Martínez de la Vega; and the cinematographers Jack Draper, Alex Phillips, and Gabriel Figueroa.

Figueroa is of special importance. His work always leaned toward ex-teriors or sequences of the countryside. Together with Emilio "El Indio" Fernández, responsible for the movies *Flor Silvestre* and *María Candelaria,* he inaugurated a black-and-white esthetic view of Mexican low-life, particularly the peasantry. He worked with John Ford and John Huston. His liaison to Cantinflas is another intriguing connection be-tween high- and low-brow art. Figueroa photographed a total of seven films of his, including *Los tres mosqueteros* (The Three Musketeers, 1942), *Un día con el diablo* (A Day with the Devil, 1945), and *El bombero atómico*

(The Atomic Fireman, 1950). Their work together marks the time in which Cantinflas was not only adored by the masses, but highly respected by the middle class and the intellectual elite. He personified Mexican street-wisdom. "In my view," Figueroa wrote in a 1990 autobiographical essay, "Mexican cinema has excelled above all in the dramatic genre, and in the antics of Cantinflas. Mario Moreno's early performances were brilliant, a marvelous portrayal of the Mexican *peladito.*" The thirties, when Cantinflas began his acting career, were a period of intense search for the clues to the nation's psyche. In 1934, Samuel Ramos, a philosophy professor at Universidad Nacional Autónoma de México, inspired by Sigmund Freud's and Alfred Adler's theories, published his influential *Profile of Man and Culture in Mexico,* a collection of interrelated essays in which he analyzed the personality of *el pelado,* as well as the urban and the bourgeois Mexican. Ramos believed Mexico was incapacitated for progress, owing to a paralyzing inferiority complex. The best way to examine the nation's soul, he argued, is through *el pelado mexicano.* He describes him as "less than proletarian and in the eyes of intellectual, a primitive. . . . [His] explosions are verbal and his lexicon is nasty and aggressive."

> We shouldn't be deceived by appearances. The pelado is neither a strong person nor a brave man. The physiognomy he exhibits is false. It's a camouflage to deceive him from those that interact with him. One could indeed establish that, the stronger and braver he behaves, the bigger the weakness he is trying to hide. . . . He lives with continual fear of being discovered, doubting himself.

Other thinkers afterwards, including Octavio Paz in *The Labyrinth of Solitude* and Roger Bartra in *The Melancholy Cage,* have expanded this argument. Although unmentioned, the early Cantinflas is always in these writer's (and their reader's) mind: a rogue, a cunning devil, an awkward citizen, a parasite. He incarnates the chaos of modern Mexican life. Can he put aside his complexes to work toward progress? Not quite: his convoluted self will always make him walk on the edge of an abyss, neither falling down nor moving away to safety. Cantinflas's Mexico: a mirror of confusion.

By the next decade, the Mexican film industry had pretty much exhausted its talents, but it was precisely in 1950 when a Spanish émigré, Luis Buñuel, produced a most astonishing film, one that would reevaluate the whole era: *Los olvidados,* a study of orphans in Mexico City pushed to a low life in crime. Buñuel was already in his late forties; the film established him, a Surrealist *enfant terrible,* as an international figure. Astonishing in numerous ways, it retains an intriguing link with Cantinflas, its cast of astute rascals openly emulating him, which, in the end, results in a masterful metamorphosis of *rascuachismo* into highbrow culture and in one more cultural theft by the haves of the have-nots. *Los olvidados* is Cantinflas for the politically sensitive, which helps explain why Cantinflas's vicissitudes beyond continental borders, particularly in the United States and Europe, are almost nonexistent. In 1956, already a monumental hero south of the Rio Grande, he was cast as Passepartout, opposite to David Niven, Buster Keaton, Frank Sinatra, and Marlene Dietrich, in *Around the World in Eighty Days* (directed by Michael Anderson). But the multistellar Hollywood movie was a total disaster. Soon after, George Sidney directed him in *Pepe* (1960). The cast included Shirley Jones, Edward G. Robinson, Zsa-Zsa Gabor, Janet Leigh, Jack Lemmon, and Kim Novak. But again, the success was limited. Although Cantinflas made the cover of *Life en español,* in Mexico and elsewhere in the Southern Hemisphere he was sharply criticized. His performances, people argued, were a death stroke to his comic capabilities. Vulgarity was his nature, why escape it? I must agree: What's remarkable about him is found in the humorous situation in the legendary *Ahí está el detalle,* where he acts as his own lawyer against a prosecutor ready to put him behind bars for a crime he didn't commit.

In his mature years, he was famous for his wealth. He had witnessed the modernization of his own country and had played a crucial role as therapeutic instrument and as millionaire. At the time of his death his personal fortune was estimated at 25 million dollars. He loved luxury, owning five mansions, the one in Mexico City containing an art gallery, a swimming pool, a jai alai fronton, a theater, a barber shop, and a beauty parlor. His private jet flew him to his thousand-acre ranch, La Purísima, where he practiced his favorite hobby, bullfighting. He was a philanthropist and each year distributed $175,000 to the homeless waiting outside his door on his birthday. He built apartment houses in the Granjas neighborhood in his nation's capital and sold them to the poor for a fraction of their worth. His high-ranking contacts in the ruling party, and he himself, often went out of their way to assure his audience that Moreno Reyes's fortune had nothing to do with drug trafficking and corruption. In *Cantinflas: Aguila o Sol,* a commemorative illustrated volume published by the government's Consejo Nacional para la Cultura y las Artes in 1993, shortly after his death, critic Carlos Bonfil time and again portrays him as an honest, self-made man, a humble, dignified Mexican—an image the state, for obvious reasons, is obsessed with safeguarding. In old age, however, Moreno Reyes was known to have close links to members of Mexico's drug cartel and to corrupt union leaders. Several million Mexicans attended his funeral (*¡El rey ha muerto!*). As time went by, Cantinflas, his creation and theirs as well, had become an immobile feature in the Mexican landscape. Like Superman and Little Orphan Annie, he never aged: his features were exactly the same from the forties to the eighties. (Moreno Reyes did gain considerable weight, but his movies never addressed this transformation.) It became obvious, at least to the ruling class, that Cantinflas could not continue as the idol of the Mexican poor simply because he had switched classes, becoming immensely rich. Rich and obese. Indeed, the whole country had grown in size: from 1938 to the early 1980s, Mexico underwent drastic changes—a massive overpopulation, growing political corruption, social injustice, the institutionalization of authority, and a student massacre. In his movies Moreno Reyes hardly addressed this metamorphosis. His Mexico was ahistorical, immutable. His protagonist was static, uninvolved, apolitical. Occasionally he does ridicule an adolescent for wearing long air or a union leader is brought to justice for incompetence, but nothing more serious or dangerous. The total government support he enjoyed early in his career translated into his own complacent silence: laughter without criticism, suffering sublimated into comedy.

By the early sixties his esthetic contribution—his championing of *rascuachismo*—had been accomplished and what followed was mere repetition: Cantinflas imitating himself in movie after movie. The status quo grew accustomed to him. His verbal usage, his civil subversion, his tasteless self, his cheap attitude, were antielitist, antiprogress, perhaps even anti-Mexican, but never against the establishment: comedy without meanness, mass appeal without aggression. Unlike Chaplin, he never exhibited any form of leftism. In fact, his canonization probably was a result of his apolitical stand: ridicule, but not aggression. So when Mexico needed to revamp its collective identity, when it looked northbound to sell another image of itself to the world, Cantinflas's *rascuachismo* was put aside: it became useless—an obstacle. Technology and education, not apathy and confusion, were now in the nation's agenda; consumerism and political stability were the accepted values, not improvisation and anarchy.

His life cycle is better understood as one realizes that when Mario Moreno Reyes entered the national scene, during the hypernationalistic period of President Lázaro Cárdenas, from 1934 to 1940, the government was preoccupied with selling an image of a peasant country in search of its pre-Columbian roots. Cárdenas expropriated foreign-held properties and oil companies, distributed land to campesinos, and instituted social reform to benefit Indians and Mexican workers. Cantinflas at the time was an irreplaceable expression of *lo mexicano*. But as the nation south of the Rio Grande moves into the twenty-first century looking northward instead of southward in search of economic, social, and political stability, another image of the country's collective spirit has emerged: enchanted with modern technology, in an eternal shopping spree, enchanted with its media image, and dressed up like the rest of Western civilization. While Cárdenas, before he was elected Mexico's president, was a general in the revolution of Pancho Villa and Emiliano Zapata, a leader in touch with the masses, contemporary presidents and their cabinet members, particularly under Carlos Salinas de Gortari's and current President Ernesto Zedillo Ponce de León's regimes, are Ivy League–educated, English-speaking deal-makers. Cárdenas has ceased to be a role model; the new inspirations are magnates and neoconservatives north of the Rio Grande, known for fortune and stability, not populist visions. And thus, Cantinflas's art, if not always remarkable in filmmaking terms, but at least always authentic, has lost the favor of the sophisticate elite, which I guess only serves to highlight the utilitarianism of the high-brow Mexican culture.

But culture is a composite, a united effort, a mosaic—the production and reproduction of symbols and motifs by upper and lower levels of society. If anything, the esthetics of *rascuachismo* highlight the enmity, the tension between rich and poor in Mexico, between Europeanized and native viewpoints. Cantinflas might be too harsh, too confronting, too conflicted an image for the bourgeoisie to accent: unwillingly, he denounces his own and everyone else's laziness, his intellectual confusion, his immature strategies to deal with modernity. Overall, he promotes a negative stereotype of *el mexicano* and might nurture fear and uncertainty toward Mexico among foreigners and "potential investors" that somehow manage to understand his verbal agitation. It's a matter of fashion, of course: to reject him, to deny his importance is to ignore the tattered, shattered, broken world of proletarian Mexico, perpetually ruptured, yet constantly stitched together and proud of itself. To discard Cantinflas, to portray him as a ruffian or parasite is to neglect one of the two halves of the Mexican self.

[1995]

FRIDA AND BENITA: UNPARALLELED LIVES

Since her death in 1954, the conversion of Frida Kahlo into a mythical figure surpassing even the stature of her abrasive husband, Diego Rivera, carries a harmful and dangerous consequence: Mexican women today are appreciated through the distorted prism of her life and *oeuvre*. Octavio Paz once described Kahlo as "a fascinating artist and complicated figure, hunted by hostile phantoms." And Carlos Fuentes suggested that she reduced Hispanic culture to her own body, "so often sacrificed and denied." But one must go further: Kahlo made art of her suffering. She used images to attempt an expurgation of her own soul and, indirectly, that of her people. Bloody wounds, a divided identity, a paralyzed, contemplative self: Is Kahlo really an allegory of femininity south of the Rio Grande? Certainly not.

Paz himself has written outstanding pages in his classic *The Labyrinth of Solitude* about womanhood in Mexico. "The Mexican woman," he writes, "quite simply has no will of her own."

> Her body is asleep and only comes really alive when someone awakens her. She is an answer rather than a question, a vibrant and easily worked material that is shaped by the imagination and sensuality of the male. In other countries women are active, attempting to attract men through the agility of their minds or the seductivity of their bodies, but the Mexican woman has a sort of hieratic calm, a tranquillity made up of both hope and contempt. The man circles around her, courts her, sings to her, sets his horse (or his imagination) to perform *caracoles* for her pleasure. Meanwhile she remains

behind the veil of her modesty and immobility. She is an idol, and like all idols she is mistress of magnetic forces whose efficacy increases as their source of transmission becomes more and more passive and secretive.

Any tourist trip to Mexico City reveals Kahlo's noxious impact on everyday life. Her portraits are endlessly reproduced in newspapers, magazines, and textbooks. Scores of quarto volumes on her art, compiled by Hayden Herrera, Raquel Tibol, and other critics, are on display in supermarkets, fashionable stores, and even in restaurants. Photographs of Frida alone and alongside Diego, her father Guillermo Kahlo, and her lover Leon Trotsky, are available as postcards. Imitations of her idiosyncratic dresses and colorful hairbands, ubiquitously on sale, have become a corrosive fashion. The painter has no doubt traveled a long road from the role of passive wife of a notorious muralist to Mexico's equivalent of Marilyn Monroe: a scandalously baroque sex symbol—the embodiment of *la mujer mexicana,* a call for rebellion, a feminist new beginning.

And yet, as part of the Europeanized minorities who have ruled Mexico since colonial times, Frida Kahlo is pure fake: a hybrid, a consummate actress. She mastered the art of adapting native costumes to her labyrinthine personality, and then resold the package to her contemporaries and the world at large. Eternally divided between her native, maternal side, and her foreign, paternal ego, she was disliked by many while alive, and other enemies have emerged since she passed away. They accuse her of reinventing the ideal of the Mexican woman, turning it from a passive, secretive transmission into a full-blown artifice.

Kahlo's authentic, unimaginative double exists under the name of Benita Galeana, an outspoken activist also closely attached to Mexico's Communist Party. They share the year of birth: 1907 (although some claim that Galeana was three years younger). One was born in the nation's capital, the other in the state of Guerrero. As Galeana's fragmented memoirs, originally written in Spanish in 1940, reprinted time and again in Hispanic America, and translated into English by Amy Diane Prince, testify, hers was a road painfully traveled. Benita transformed herself from an abused and seduced rural girl to a high-ranking freedom-fighter, from anonymous sufferer to famous associate of José Clemente Orozco, José Revueltas, and Fidel Castro.

Aside from Kahlo, whom Galeana wholeheartedly detested, the neighboring nation south of the border has a shamefully short list of forthright, candid women, fictional and otherwise. The roster might include Hernán Cortés's mistress and translator La Malinche, the poet Sor Juana Inés de la Cruz, the wife of the *corregidor* of Querétaro, Josefa Ortíz de Domínguez, the Italian photographer Tina Modotti, Elena Poniatowska's well-known character Jesusa Palancares, and, of course, the ever-present Virgin of Guadalupe. Benita Galeana no doubt ranks high among them. Her autobiography is an invaluable document crucial to understanding ideological dissent in Mexico since the Partido Revolucionario Institucional came to power in 1929, a testament of the resistance and affirmation of Hispanic women throughout the twentieth century.

No human life is truly individual. Our acts are repetitious and fit within preconceived patterns. Galeana's odyssey is not unlike those of Danton and Robespierre, Rev. Martin Luther King, Jr., David ben Gurion, Lech Walesa, and Rigoberta Menchú. Her chapters are marked by the sudden death of her mother, poverty, her father's alcoholism, syndicalism and the joining of forces with urban workers, persecution by the Pascual Ortiz Rubio and Abelardo Rodríguez regimes, imprisonment, and torture. She was still a young girl when the lifeless body of José Guadalupe Posada was buried in a collective grave. At the time she learned about the revolts of Emiliano Zapata and Pancho Villa. Unfortunately, time has a way of ridiculing her past. As an adult, Benita Galeana repeatedly made the wrong ideological allegiances: she befriended Orozco, she belittled Lázaro Cárdenas and then applauded his son Cuauhtémoc, she kissed her idol Fidel Castro in Havana, she even adored Panama's General Manuel Antonio Noriega.

Alongside Pablo Neruda and many others, Benita Galeana was part of an ill-fated generation of Latin American left-wingers who saw hope in dogmatism and utopia in tyranny. She remained a devoted Marxist long after the fall of the Berlin Wall and the Balkanization of the U.S.S.R. But in spite of her stubbornness, in spite of her ideological and sexual temptations and her nearsightedness, Benita remains an attractive emblem owing to her infinite courage. Indeed, her liaisons map an invaluable journey by women in Mexico from the periphery of culture and politics to centerstage. It is no accident that the Taller de Gráfica Popular, Carlos Monsiváis, and cartoonist Abel Quezada pay tribute to her. Unlike the average Mexican female of her era, Benita's body was never asleep. She was not an answer rather than a question, and was never shaped by the imagination and sensuality of the country's male. Hers was not a hieratic calm, a tranquility made up of both hope and contempt. While she managed to outlive Frida Kahlo by over four decades, Galeana's achievement was never histrionic. She might have dressed as an *acateca* or *tehuana,* but her costumes were never staged mannerisms.

Given our present-day insatiable thirst for exhibitionism, given the complexities of Mexico's collective identity, it is not at all surprising to me that Benita Galeana, and not Kahlo, remains a shadowy figure, a footnote in history.

[1994]

CARLOS FUENTES IN HIS LABYRINTH

Carlos Fuentes is a seasoned postmodern ventriloquist. His trademark is his talent to adapt other people's work. He navigates under the banner of multiculturalism, shaping his persona as a plurinational hybrid (he was born in Panama City in 1928, the son of a Mexican diplomat, and raised on the River Plate and in Washington, D.C.). Using the novel, his favorite genre, as an anything-goes container, the crossroads where history, philosophy, literary criticism, and popular culture intersect, Fuentes inspires scholars to celebrate him as an overwhelming Renaissance man and championing his cosmopolitan vision. But beyond obligatory college readings, his audience, mostly a remnant of a bygone decade when Latin American letters mattered in Europe and the United States, is rapidly shrinking. Fuentes seems to have saturated the world with his repetitiveness.

As Chandler Brossard once observed, Fuentes has an insatiable thirst for seeing his name in print. He is frequently quoted on nearly every topic and current event: the campesino uprising in Chiapas, sex, tyranny and democracy among Hispanics, the Balkanization of Eastern Europe, French politics, First Amendment rights, the 1993 Nobel Prize for Literature to Toni Morrison, and a long et cetera. His charisma and ubiquitous facial gesture of concern (his Emiliano Zapata mustache often makes him look angry and annoyed) pay off in lecture tours on the university circuit. And yet despite his formidable gifts as a fiction writer and cultural commentator, lately he seems unable to create moving scenes. His recent creations are flat, cartoonlike, idle proxies for allegorical truths.

The most suitable adjective to describe his writing is cumulative. His narratives add information and append secondary characters, keeping a small leitmotif that leads to a sepulchral center. In order to reach the heart of a Fuentes text, the reader needs to excavate, to distinguish between details of significance and dispensable data, an exhausting exercise that seldom pays off. A sideboard of Fuentes's obsessions is his newest collection of stories, *The Orange Tree,* originally published in Spain in early 1993. Biculturalism and a dual identity are at the core. Three of the five narratives have the word *two* in the title. In one way or another, every one deals with a Dr. Jekyll and Mr. Hyde division: two sons claiming the right to represent their father's legacy; a sailor connecting two abysmally distant continents; an Iberian chronicler loyal to two patrons, metaphorically as well as physically. Echoes of numerous writers are heard at every turn. At the outset, for instance, is a tale about a Spanish contemporary of Bernal Díaz del Castillo in the conquest of Tenochtitlán in 1523 that uses a regressive structure with resonance of Harold Pinter and A. B. Yehoshua. "Son of the Conquistador," the second entry, about the heirs of Hernán Cortés, two men named Martín, one the Creole child of a Native American, the other a *gachupín* in the Iberian Peninsula, cannot be read without invoking William Faulkner. "Apollo and the Whores," about a Hollywood actor looking for an adventurous death who ultimately meets his end in Acapulco, is written in diary form, recalling the art of Claude Simon and Gabriel García Márquez. Concluding the volume is a first-person account by a Columbus open about his Sephardic blood, inspired by the Cuban musicologist and writer Alejo Carpentier's *The Harp and the Shadow,* as well as works by Paul Claudel and Nikos Kazantzakis.

Many threads connect the five tales, ranging from a passing reference to an orange tree to biographical allusions ending a story and emerging in the next, to sensual pleasures at the core of single plots—sights, touch, taste. Such everlasting reverberance of literary voices is meant to represent Fuentes as a portable library, a metaliterary, ahistorical dialogue wherein a confabulation of authors from the twentieth century, dead and alive, talk to each other. Certainly Fuentes has to be applauded for his incredible stamina. He is no doubt a very intelligent writer whose extraordinary esthetic and political odyssey allows us to understand Latin America's modern search for identity. He manages to publish a book almost every year, which probably explains the essentially dissatisfying quality of his later prose. To quote Yogi Berra, one cannot avoid a feeling of "déjà vu all over again."

Most of Fuentes's oeuvre is available to U.S. readers, and a few titles, including *The Death of Artemio Cruz,* have even been translated twice because of the inefficacy of the first attempt. Only marginal facets of his career remain obscure north of the border. (His screenwriting, for instance: among his film projects, he collaborated in adapting Juan Rulfo's *Pedro Páramo.*) His essay collections, including one on Mexican politics in the late sixties and another on the new Latin American novel, remain largely untranslated. Similarly, some nonfiction texts drafted in English, mainly the autobiographical ones, are unknown to Hispanic audiences. While as literary critic Fuentes oscillates between a fragile coherence and flashes of portentous intellect, he remains his own best interpreter. In the first part of *Myself with Others,* his 1988 collection of essays that reads as a tribute to Philip Roth (in fact, the volume is dedicated to the Jewish-American novelist and his then-spouse, Claire Bloom), is about his own pilgrimage as a writer and the shaping of his best work, *Aura,* a gothic novella. Still a best-seller in the Spanish-speaking world, *Aura* stands as an exercise in self-restraint, an attitude quite rare in Fuentes. No doubt a signature of late-twentieth-century fiction, everywhere one looks today one finds books talking about books, writers metamorphosing into other writers. The problem with Fuentes is that he did his best metaliterary work decades ago. *Aura*'s refreshing luminosity is far gone. He now appears lost in the labyrinth of his own verbosity.

At this point in his career, Columbus, Moctezuma, and Hernán Cortés are Fuentes's favorite archetypes, all of whom have a role in *The Orange Tree.* In "The Two Americas," Jews and Muslim Arabs (another of Fuentes's perennial subjects) are reconsidered in the shaping of Columbus's life and legacy; and the link between Spain and the New World, explored in Fuentes's subjective historical volume *The Buried Mirror,* where he lays down what he likes and dislikes about Hispanic culture, is a subject apparent everywhere in the collection. Nothing new, then, in Fuentes's literary carousel.

I once heard Fuentes claim that he had very little respect for critics, portraying himself as a cannibal who chews on the bones of his attackers and then throws them away. Forty years after his first collection of stories, *Los días enmascarados,* was first published in Mexico, negative views of his oeuvre abound. Feminists often accuse him of misrepresenting Hispanic women. And the last time a book of his was reviewed in *The New Republic,* the Mexican historian Enrique Krauze, an Octavio Paz acolyte, painted him as a charlatan, which stirred a majestic controversy south of the Rio Grande, where Fuentes is considered a sacred cow among intolerant supporters. In front-page articles, loyal columnists indicted Krauze as an unsympathetic Jew who dared to ridicule the author of *Old Gringo* beyond national borders. Many even saw Krauze's action as a maneuver by Paz, once Fuentes's friend and now an acerbic enemy, to retain the attention needed to capture the Nobel Prize for Literature, which he received in 1990. Months of debate were followed by Fuentes's silence. Not a single word did he utter.

Rather than trusting others to interpret his work, Fuentes enjoys being his own critic. Since *Christopher Unborn,* his 1987 novel á la Laurence Sterne, the Spanish edition of his books includes a page, called "The Ages of Times," in which he offers unity and cleavage to his work, portraying every title as another installment in a larger-than-life oeuvre that could easily pay homage to Balzac's *Comédie humaine.* As years go by, he lists written and unwritten works, and the titles keep on changing. *The Orange Tree,* absent before in this list, appears at the very end, subtitled "The Cycles of Time," dropped in the English translation by Alfred MacAdam. And indeed, the five stories in the volume retain a cyclical configuration. We begin with the fall of Tenochtitlán and end with a transhistorical Christopher Columbus signing a contractual concession to a Japanese corporation for T-shirts, fried chicken, pizzas, cameras, and stereos to be marketed as a result of his so-called discovery of Paradise. Implicit in each story is a critical tone through which Fuentes invites the reader to appreciate the text's other side, an interpretive device, deliberately anachronistic, meant to help understand the writer's intention. Fuentes is portraying himself as a completely self-sufficient literary entity—a one-man army, part medium to historical and fictional figures, part autocritic, and part gluttonous reader.

None of the stories in *The Orange Tree* leaves a mark in the reader's memory. They are easily confused and forgotten. Fuentes injects in their chemistry something histrionic, depriving them of any trace of humility, a quality Fuentes himself has perfected in the staged persona he builds as a fortress evident in his lectures. His English is impeccable and his charm, a consummate artifice. The message is less attractive than the messenger. His stories suffer from the same abundance of gesture and ingenuousness. As I read them, I couldn't help wondering where the writer was, that vulnerable entity with doubts and uncertainties.

Augusto Monterroso, a Guatemalan fabulist still awaiting a U.S. readership, once wrote a speculative text about writers dating their stories. He notes that essays, especially those dealing with current affairs, need a chronological frame of reference for the reader to know what was and wasn't available during composition. But stories aiming at universality are allergic to such down-to-earth precision, which means that dating fiction, he concludes, is pointless. Fuentes illustrates Monterroso's point admirably. Every text in *The Orange Tree,* written between 1991 and 1992, is dated in a different locality: London, Mexico, Spain's El Escorial, Valdemorillo-Formentor, and Acapulco. In case anyone fails to notice, the Mexican takes very seriously his role as cultural diplomat of the Hispanic world, a wandering ghost occasionally appearing at a symposium in his honor, a gala dinner to support Salman Rushdie, an interview with Bill Moyers, or as host of a television series: a total man, digesting every stimulus accessible, a ventriloquist mouthing other people's voices. The result of his fancifulness, his bombardment of data, is a sense of abuse felt among his readers. *The Orange Tree* fails as good literature because it's more interested in making a point than in offering an insight into human understanding. It is about humans but lacks humanity.

When readers in the next millennium recapitulate the narrative achievements of our fin de siècle, a handful of conclusions are likely to emerge. First, World War II brought along the rotation of obscure national literatures from the periphery of culture to center stage, which meant that V. S. Naipaul, Nadine Gordimer, and Anita Desai were possible once Europe ceased to be exclusive. Second, the proliferation of translations and seminars worldwide made bizarre connections among writers uniting Borges with Danilo Kiš and John Barth with the Brazilian modernist Joaquím María Machado de Asís. Third, and most important, people got a feeling of what Emerson and Coleridge envisioned at least 150 years before: In spite of the diversity readers got by reading authors from distant regions in the late 1990s, the spirit of an all-encompassing Writer of Writers dictating every single sentence in multiple languages was felt when one pondered the ideas of originality and transmogrification. All this might persuade audiences in the twenty-first century that Carlos Fuentes was simultaneously the perfect hybrid and consummate cultural androgyne. An envoy of the so-called Third World, he made audiences in developed countries ashamed of their ignorance while proving, once and for all, that you can be Hispanic *and* cosmopolitan, a citizen from a barbarous civilization offering a lesson to ignorant readers in Europe and the United States. He attempted to become a mirror of the Writer of Writers on earth, a know-it-all, do-it-all creative machine. People north of the Rio Grande and across the Atlantic believed him because they mistakenly trusted that articulate, multifaceted Latin Americans like him were an endangered species, an exception to the rule. Consequently, it was next to impossible for them to read a Mexican writer interested in small realistic scenes and averse to archetypal images about repression and imperialism. But while Fuentes's prodigious output might lead many to believe he was a genius, future readers will also conclude that his overall contribution was tarnished by a gargantuan appetite and a Hollywood persona. His early work, guided by a principle of self-restraint, remains unforgettable.

[1994]

JOSÉ GUADALUPE POSADA: A PROFILE

Since the turn of the century, political cartoons and murals in Mexico have been considered forms of street art. Still a highly cultivated medium, political cartoons were published from the 1850s on in prints and chapbooks that captured the imagination of the masses—rarely the sophisticated, highly literate elite. Like journalistic accounts, they offered quick insight into contemporary affairs, and then they perished. In the decades before the socialist revolution of 1910, millions were enlightened and entertained by Jose Guadalupe Posada's lurid, eye-catching, marvelous engravings, which were often accompanied by jocular lyrics. Murals, on the other hand, were less ephemeral, more detailed and colorful. In the thirties, the busy passerby might see aspects of Mexico's history painted from a Marxist point of view in murals by Diego Rivera, David Alfaro Siqueiros, and José Clemente Orozco. While Posada was incapable of seeing the pedagogic possibilities of muralism as a form of political activism, preferring to rely on the graphic arts to educate the populace, Rivera and his circle later acknowledged their debt to Posada's hyperbolic illustrations, both in their art and their writings, and by doing so created a bridge between the two forms of street art.

But Posada, it seems to me, was more than just a populist artist. He invented the most fascinating freaks and grotesque monstrosities, and in that regard he is comparable to Goya, Rudolph von Ripper, Alfred Kubin, Sibylle Ruppert, and the creators of the fabulous beasts and demons of the medieval and Renaissance worlds.

Posada was born on February 2, 1852, at number 47 Calle de Los Angeles (later Calle de Posada) in the city of Aguascalientes in central Mexico. (Some encyclopedias give his year of birth as 1851.) The fourth of six—some sources say eight—children, of which only three survived, he was baptized in the Parroquia de la Asunción. Both of his parents were of Indian descent and illiterate. Germán Posada, his father, was a baker who owned a small shop; Petra Aguilar, his mother, was a housewife. Their oldest son, José María de la Concepción, died when still a child. The second, José Cirilo, born in 1839, became a schoolteacher. He taught José Guadalupe to read and write, until the latter and his younger brother Ciriaco were sent to a municipal school in the San Marcos neighborhood. Apparently, Posada enjoyed drawing even as a child, for he made humorous portraits of José Cirilo and his young pupils. Unfortunately, none of these early artistic experiments can be found.

As an adolescent, Posada studied with Antonio Varela at the Municipal Academy of Drawing in Aguascalientes. By 1867 he began practicing the "trade of the painter," and the following year he apprenticed in the lithography workshop of Trinidad Pedroza. Politically active, Pedroza supported the creation of a local government and spoke out against the ineffectiveness of city politicians—particularly the influential Colonel Jesús Gómez Portugal—and the economic and military intervention of France and the United States in Mexican affairs. In addition to lithography, Posada learned the basic printmaking techniques of engraving wood and metal. He also began producing lampoons and illustrations for magazines and books, selling some to Pedroza's own independent newspaper, *El Jicote*. Many of them featured Colonel Portugal as their main target.

Biographical information is scarce, so it is impossible to say precisely when or how Posada's political conscience was awakened. Some, like Octavio Paz, Mexico's foremost contemporary essayist and poet, claim that Posada's ideology has actually been misunderstood. According to Paz, Posada's work was not the prototype of *el arte de protesta* but simply a recording of what he saw. Since the artist was surrounded by the poor and uneducated, his subject matter just happened to look "progressive." Paz, however, wrongly oversimplifies Posada's artistic spirit. While it is true that political manifestoes do not exist in his oeuvre—the tracts of Pierre Joseph Proudhon and scientific socialism not having reached him from Europe—he had a "socialist" *weltanschauung* and always expressed a strong social conscience. Even without a specific message, in image after image Posada clearly condemns injustice. And while he may not

José Guadalupe Posada, *¡Caso raro! Una mujer que
dio a luz tres niños y cuatro animales* ("A rare case! A
woman gives birth to three children and four animals"). Zinc etching (detail), Library of Congress,
Prints and Photographs Division, Swann Collection.

have subscribed to a particular philosophical or governmental remedy
for the ills of his epoch, his lampoons nevertheless are testimony to the
inequities and instabilities of his fragile country.

At times his stand regarding certain public figures is ambiguous. He
could support the president and condemn his enemies, only to ridicule
the ruler later. And, as mentioned, politics or political figures were by no
means the focus of his lampooning. Folklore and "magical" happenings,
subjects popular with everyone, provided ample grist for his cartoons.
Regardless of his choice of subject, though, Posada was unmistakably
allied with the dispossessed.

The subversive element in Posada's work is humor—an ingredient that makes his images as compelling today as they were in his time. Through humor, Posada denounced delinquency, assassinations, and corruption. Through humor, he sympathetically described the struggles of popular heroes. According to Paz, Posada's comic equivalent is the French playwright Alfred Jarry, himself a creator of popular prints, who drew inspiration for the absurd world of his King Ubu from Posada's imagery. Although both are rooted in the nineteenth century, they are also our contemporaries, Paz claims, and will be contemporaries of our children through the timeless appeal of their humor.

Even in his earliest works, Posada is a satirist. While maintaining loyalty to his visual perceptions, he never forgets to inject a comic element. There is a hint of the Rabelaisian—or better, Quevedesque—touch that he would later perfect. Usually his early images synthesized an accompanying text or interpreted it with stereotypes and symbols. At this point in his career, he had not yet developed the distinct style of his later works. Perceiving his craft as a means of graphically, but not always sensuously, explaining the daily news, he printed portraits of diplomats, demons, virgins, lawyers, and bankers, and depicted comets, natural disasters, and national events.

While Benito Juárez, a pure-blooded Indian lawyer, was Mexico's president, *El Jicote*, with its constant criticism of politicians and the establishment, angered the local authorities and was forced to close. Nineteen-year-old Posada was considered a political agitator. He and Pedroza realized that they had to leave Aguascalientes as soon as possible, so together they went to the city of León de los Aldamas in the state of Guanajuato, where they opened a commercial lithographic business in 1872. It was a prosperous and very religious city, and Posada made a living mainly from producing Christian stamps, as well as cards, invitations, stickers, and labels for cigar packages and liquor bottles. For the time being, politics were left behind.

In 1873 Pedroza returned to Aguascalientes, and Posada was left in charge of the shop. Although he knew that he was not a good businessman, Posada enjoyed being his own boss. In 1875 he married María de Jesús Varela. (He had a son but not by his wife. The boy died in his teens.) All in all, the future looked bright. A terrible flood, however, devastated León in 1887, and Posada lost everything. In 1888 he moved with his family to Mexico City, where he opened a workshop downtown, on Calle

José Guadalupe Posada, *Esta es de Don Quijote la primera, la sin par, la gigante calavera* ("This one is of Don Quixote, the best, the incomparable, the gigantic skeleton"). Type-metal engraving, Library of Congress, Prints and Photographs Division, Swann Collection.

de Santa Teresa and subsequently on Calle Santa Inés (later Emiliano Zapata).

While the history of muralism in Mexico has been well researched, lithography has been relatively neglected. Early on, the technique was used primarily to illustrate scientific treatises, but largely owing to the influence of the French artist Honoré Daumier, it quickly became a popular artistic medium. Mexico's first lithographic workshop was established in 1826 by Claudio Linati and used to produce the newspaper *El Iris*. Posada was familiar with the prints of early Mexican lithographers such as J. M. Villasana, Hipólito Salazar, and Santiago Hernández. Close scrutiny of his images, though, reveals that he also was acquainted with the work of a handful of European avant-garde artists, specifically Edgar Degas, Edouard Manet, and Henri de Toulouse-Lautrec.

In Mexico City, Posada made contact with the artist and engraver Manuel Manilla, who introduced him to Antonio Vanegas Arroyo, an editor and publisher of street gazettes and a true pioneer of modern journalism. Arroyo recognized not only Posada's artistic talent but also his prodigious drive; he offered to hire him, with a promise of complete artistic freedom. Posada sold his own shop and began a prolific career with Arroyo, producing hundreds of thousands of cartoons, love letters, school books, card games, penny dreadfuls, and commercial advertisements like posters for circus performances or bull fights.

On occasion, Posada would illustrate satirical verses or simple news reports written by Arroyo or Constancio Suárez, a poet from the state of Oaxaca. The trio of editor, illustrator, and poet became a very famous and extremely productive and powerful voice until 1895, when Suárez died. Posada and Arroyo continued their partnership, and with the benefit of Arroyo's entrepreneurial spirit, Posada reached millions with his images, becoming a spokesman for Mexico's collective soul.

It is commonly thought that during his association with Arroyo, Posada created the *calavera*—a humorous, vivid drawing of dressed-up skulls or skeletons engaged in activities such as dancing, cycling, guitar playing, drinking, or masquerading. In fact, it was Manuel Manilla who first drew these fanciful characters, publishing *calaveras* in newspapers and street gazettes as early as 1883. Posada, however, was the one who popularized them, and thus he is often mistakenly credited with their invention.

In a European context, *calaveras* derive from the medieval imagery of the *danse macabre,* or Dance of Death. Peter Wollen dates the tradition to fresco paintings of the fifteenth century and then to a series of woodcuts by Hans Holbein in 1538. Posada so personalized the imagery, though, his *calaveras* have become metaphors for his homeland: they are to Mexico what Uncle Sam is to the United States. Originally, Posada simply intended to commemorate Mexico's Day of the Dead on November 2, when the poor and illiterate picnic and sleep in cemeteries to be close to their beloved dead. But the *calaveras* were immensely popular. They captivated audiences by poking fun at the adventures of Cervantes's *Don Quixote* or José Zorrilla's play *Don Juan Tenorio.* Now, sculptural sugar *calaveras* are consumed every year to celebrate the holiday. Later generations of artists were also influenced by the macabre characters, including Orozco, who, like Posada, started his career as a cartoonist, and Rivera. Rivera's mural *Dream of a Sunday Afternoon in Alameda Park,* in Mexico City's now-destroyed Hotel del Prado, depicts a female *calavera catrina,* a society belle, wearing a scarf and hat. To the skeleton's left, arm-in-arm with her, stands Posada; to her right is Frida Kahlo, Rivera's tormented mistress, and a childish self-portrait of the muralist himself.

Many of Posada's *calaveras* bear no signature, and over the years the works of countless imitators and forgers have been falsely attributed to him. Even images like *Calavera huertista* or *Calavera zapatista,* both possibly the creation of Manilla, have sometimes been mistakenly ascribed to Posada.

Posada became a master of the chiaroscuro. Overcoming the limitations of engraving and lithography, he injected his images with force and passion. Antonio Rodríguez explains Posada's primary printmaking techniques in his book *Posada: The Man Who Portrayed an Epoch:*

> Before settling in Mexico [City] Posada had used the technique of the lithograph. When he went to work for Arroyo . . . , he needed to find a more suitable method for clear, spectacular illustrations that were sharp in line and could be rapidly reproduced. With this in mind he adapted a method already in use in the workshop which consisted of

engraving drawings on a plates of lead or an alloy of lead and zinc, almost as in wood engraving.

Among the tools he used . . . were various types of burin, among them the "velo," or multiple-line tool rather like the teeth of a saw, the various points and grooves of which produced parallel tracks on the surface of the plate.

Later, under the pressure to compete with newspapers that were using modern photo-engraving procedures, Posada . . . [replaced] the burin with a combination of varnishes and acids.

With the old technique, the engraver opened grooves in the plate (of wood and metal), knowing that only what was not engraved . . . would be printed on the paper. With the new technique, the artist drew or painted his sketches with a pen or brush dipped in protective varnish, and when the other parts of the sheet were eaten away on dipping the sheet in acid, the sketch remained intact for printing. . . . [This method] is rapid and allows great freedom.

Political cartoons and idiosyncratic comic strips are immensely popular throughout Mexico, and Posada is considered the founding father of the genre. Every significant historic event of his epoch appears in his cartoons. He ridiculed the dictatorship of Porfirio Díaz, a mixed-blooded general from Oaxaca who fought the French invasion in the 1860s, whereby Napoleon III installed the Austrian Archduke Maximilian of Hapsburg as emperor of Mexico. At first appearing to be a progressive liberal, Díaz led an abortive coup against the charismatic president Benito Juárez in 1871. He organized another revolt and eventually became president, ruling Mexico tyrannically from 1876 to 1911 except for one four-year term. Posada also made fun of Mexico's huge foreign debt and of the colonization of Cuba by the United States. He lampooned his country's bourgeoisie for their arrogance and used sensational canards to stir up additional excitement.

When the revolution began, Posada was fifty-eight years old and had produced fifteen thousand engravings. He was a supporter of Francisco Madero, a wealthy lawyer who militarily opposed Díaz and became president in 1911—only to be murdered two years later by one of his men,

Victoriano Huerta. He also sympathized with Emiliano Zapata, a guerrilla from the state of Morelos who fought for the peasants and agrarian
reform. During these years, Posada's engravings depict national heroes
and symbols, such as women soldiers. Jean Charlot, one of the artist's
dedicated admirers, wrote, "The Revolution was a Posada 'still' come to
life, its tableaux charted by his able brown hand before it had even begun." Unfortunately, he did not live to see the end of the conflict.

In 1910, around the time that his wife died, Posada created another
famous character, Don Chepito Marihuano, a middle-class bachelor who
counterbalanced Posada's satiric, at times cruel, voice with a moralistic
one. Because of his strong influence with his audiences, Posada may have
had apprehensions about providing criticisms without solutions. De-
parting from his customary pessimism, the artist took a positive approach, using Don Chepito to persuade the ignoramus to adopt civic
manners. Don Chepito made fun of social foibles but afterward offered
a pedagogic message. His every appearance was educational, with rules
regarding behavior, ethics, and honor.

For more than twenty years, Posada lived in a poor neighborhood
near the Tepito market, at number 6 Avenida de la Paz (later Jesus
Carranza). It was there that he died, penniless, on January 20, 1913, of
gastroenteritis. He was buried in a pauper's grave in the Dolores cemetery. Seven years later, after no one had claimed his mortal remains, his
bones were exhumed and tossed in a communal grave. While not uncommon, the mass burial can be seen as a metaphor for Posada's anonymity.

Posada embodied Mexico's renaissance in his perception of the country as independent of Europe and in his desire to establish a national art
with indigenous motifs and symbols dating to the Conquest. National
and international events parade through his imagery: the awaited earthquake of 1899, which was considered an omen of the apocalypse; the
burning of a library in Chicago; the famous criminal trial of María
Antonia Rodríguez, who was accused of killing her *compadre.* His political heroes were bandits and Robin Hoods; and his political cartoons
express concepts and themes later expounded in Mexican murals. Within
his simple and sometimes static images, he displays a considerable
amount of inventiveness and fantasy, as in the cartoon of a woman who
gives birth to three children and four animals, or the one of a girl with a

face on her buttocks. One could argue that Posada foreshadows elements of the so-called magic realism style of literature—with its dramatic juxtapositions of reality and fantasy—as embodied in the writings of Gabriel García Márquez and Juan Rulfo.

Posada's imagery was so varied, his burin so prolific that it is difficult to know how best to approach his body of work. Roberto Bardecio and Stanley Appelbaum have established a thematic hierarchy: *calaveras,* disasters, national events, religion and miracles, Don Chepito Marihuano, chapbook covers, chapbook illustrations, everyday life, and miscellaneous prints. One could also approach his oeuvre chronologically and biographically, examining the art as it developed in the context of his life. Or, one can simply ignore any logical sequence and approach the work chaotically—which is my preference. The artist is best appreciated when external frameworks are not imposed on him. His spirit erupts in each autonomous engraving or lithograph, and the encounter between image and viewer is pure pleasure.

Posada's life after death was yet another act of creation. He did not find an immediate following. For the next decade, the Academia de Bellas Artes de San Carlos, a national institute founded in 1778 to preserve traditions and techniques in the visual arts, ignored emerging indigenous trends in favor of imported styles and ideas. To counterattack this, the Taller de Gráfica Popular was formed in 1937 under the socialist regime of Lázaro Cárdenas. The group supported new artistic movements and tried collectively to create a revolutionary street art. At the same time, the so-called Mexican school—in particular Rivera and Orozco—frequently produced lithographs strongly influenced by Posada. Together with Emilio Amero, Jean Charlot, Miguel Covarrubias, Carlos Mérida, Pablo O'Higgins, and Rufino Tamayo, the two muralists created a lithographic tradition of great impact following the teachings of Posada.

Two sources might be credited with restoring Posada to prominence. In 1920, the early modernist painter Dr. Alt (Gerardo V. Murillo) "rediscovered" Posada. It was Jean Charlot, however, a French immigrant to Mexico and a friend of the muralists, who showed around Posada's prints and wrote about him during the twenties in the context of Cubism. He brought the engraver to the attention of Rivera, Orozco, and Siqueiros, who were so enchanted with his artistic spirit that they embraced him as their master. Rivera once stated that Posada "was so closely associated with the spirit of the Mexican people that he may end up just as an abstraction"—in other words, his legacy would become a collective one, which has indeed happened. Orozco saw Posada as one of the greatest artists, one "able to teach an admirable lesson in simplicity, humility, equilibrium and dignity."

In *Posada: Messenger of Mortality,* Peter Wollen analyzes Posada in Borgesian fashion: through the eyes of his successors. He examines, for example, similarities between him and the early European avant-gardist Gustave Courbet—a painter of earthy, and sometimes crude, realism— and he discusses the affection some of the Cubists, such as Piet Mondrian, had for the Mexican cartoonist because of their re-evaluation of noncanonical and "primitive" forms of art. Wollen also refers to Posada's influence on Russian *lubki*—posters and small books containing ballads, tales, and tracts—made by Mikhail Larionov and other Golden Fleece and Donkey's Tail artists. Larionov knew of Posada through his friend Rivera, whom he frequently visited in Paris.

Other cultural links can be found, such as Posada's appeal to the Russian director Sergei Mikhailovich Eisenstein and to Surrealists such as Alfred Jarry and André Breton, who cherished the *calavera* for its cruel, yet humorous, morbidity. In an enthusiastic article, Breton wrote that:

> the rise of humor in art to a clear, pure form seems
> to have taken place in a period very close to our own.
> Its foremost practitioner is the Mexican artist Posada
> who, in his wonderful popular engravings, brings
> home to us all the conflicts of the 1910 Revolution.
> . . . They tell us something about the passage of
> comedy from speculation to action and remind us
> that Mexico, with its superb funereal playthings, is the
> chosen land of black humor.

According to Wollen, Eisenstein first saw Posada's work in Berlin in 1929, at the house of playwright Ernst Toller. The Russian filmmaker, himself an aspiring artist, shared the Mexican printmaker's interest in crowds, revolution, and tumultuous events, as seen in his movies such as the 1925 *Battleship Potemkin, October,* which was made in 1927, and the unfinished *¡Qué viva México!* In his autobiography *Immortal Memories,* Eisenstein explains how, when learning to draw, his drawing went through a stage of purification in his striving for a mathematically abstract and pure line, and how he was influenced at the time by Rivera, Mexican primitivism, and the "cheap prints" of Posada.

In what may be the ultimate praise, Rivera compared Posada to Francisco de Goya. In drawing his analogy, Rivera had the artists' populism in mind. But, as I argued before, the links between the enlightened eighteenth-century Spaniard and the pre-modernist Mexican are even more obvious, at least at one level: both created an enduring zoology of imaginary beings. Rivera wrote of Posada:

> Entirely original, Posada's work speaks with a pure
> Mexican accent. . . . If we accept August Renoir's
> dictum that the true work of art is "indefinable and
> inimitable," we can safely say that Posada's engravings
> are works of art of the highest order. Posada can
> never be imitated; he can never be defined. In terms
> of technique, his work is pure plasticity; in terms of
> content, it is life itself: two things that cannot be
> imprisoned in the straitjacket of a definition.

Rivera loved the Posada of the urban poor, the lumpen street people. But equally enjoyable, and most attractive to me, is the Posada who transports us to a universe of gothic, at times grotesque, magical, and bizarre incidents, or Posada the anarchist, dwelling on catastrophe, satire, and death. Death, in fact, is his primary preoccupation, as far as I am concerned—not an existential, painful death, but one that is irrevocable, social, and egalitarian. The gothic facet of Posada has, unfortunately, gone unattended. His universe is full of bats, griffins, skeletons, animal hybrids, snakes, explosions, pistols, demons, ghosts, and deformities. He draws attention to fear, despair, and criminality. His monsters are not pure abstraction; they are symbols, allegorical images, metaphors. They have a life of their own yet are tied to the human reality. They deserve a place next to the sphinx, the multiple-headed dragon, and the behemoth, as well as Pieter Brueghel's vision of Hell. Posada was able to portray the sadism, torture, madness, superstition, and paranoia of his time through these incredibly complex, outstandingly imaginative characters without ever losing touch with the Mexican soul, perhaps, because they inhabit it.

Why is this master of street art relevant today? Because he was a genius without artifice or pomposity. Because he truly spoke to the masses. Because he was attracted to the calamitous and absurd, as mankind will always be. Because rarely does an artist manage to bridge the gap between popular and sophisticated tastes as he did through his lampoons and cartoons. To put it simply, because Posada *is* Mexico.

[1990]

SEÑORA RODRÍGUEZ'S PURSE

Of the appetite for whimsical, bizarre entanglements in the Latin American novel there is little doubt. What human circumstance hasn't been explored and exploited? What tiny and inconsequential aspect of life remains untouched? From the isolation of El Supremo to the annunciations of Remedios La Bella, from the diary of an embryo in Carlos Fuentes to the totemization of the penis in José Lezama Lima and the instruction manual for ascending a staircase by Julio Cortázar, not a single slice of life, not a recondite behavioral pattern has gone unnoticed. Every demeanor, it seems, every grotesque thought is suitable in the Southern Hemisphere for novelistic pyrotechnics. Indeed, it often seems ironic that a civilization so nearsighted and uncritical in its political sphere should be so plenteous, so gluttonous in its literary endeavors. The explanation, of course, is that dreams and dreams alone is what the region is about: It was a utopian reverie that brought the continent to life, and it is an impossible hope that keeps it afloat. Dreams are to its inhabitants like bread and water. Small surprise, then, that the female novelists, whose rise to prominence was a result of the liberating sixties, would turn the domestic realm—kitchen recipes, a baby crying, a family photo album—into the field of dreams. No reductionism meant here, though: literary women south of the Rio Grande are as eager and qualified to unravel the contradictions of our indecipherable universe as their male counterparts; but they are also more likely to do so while fixing a leaking faucet or crossing out items on a supermarket list.

This talent, the act of making the mundane exemplary, is articulated quite well in *Señora Rodríguez and Other Worlds*, a delightful miniature of a novel, an Escher-like game by Martha Cerda. Daydreaming is what the book is about. Señora Rodríguez, the protagonist, does nothing but daydream; this is her sport, her *raison d'être*. She is not really a person but a Platonic universal, all the mothers and housewives and daughters-in-law in the world condensed into one. What makes her unique is that her daydreams are circular and self-referential; that is, she daydreams that she daydreams that she daydreams . . . thereby keeping herself constantly busy. I mean busy to the point of immobility. The novel has no real action to speak of. It is made of a single scene, constantly repeated in various time-frames: always the same Señora Rodríguez, age fifty-five, elegant and well-regarded, reaching into her purse with her left hand to find . . . well, all sorts of junk. Nothing more happens. It is the junk that creates the novelistic suspense, inviting marvelous reflections on identity: a half-licked lollipop, Kleenex, a pair of glasses, contraceptives, a set of photos. . . . These items remind Señora Rodríguez that she is alive and well and in the process of becoming, although what she is actually becoming is very hard for her to say. As the reader moves on, the junk becomes more abstract. It ceases to have direct link to the concrete, outside world and is transformed into a metaphor. At one point, for instance, Señora Rodríguez reaches into her purse to find her own soul; and a few scenes later, in an obvious homage to Don Quixote, she finds the very manuscript of *Señora Rodríguez and Other Worlds* and what else but us readers. By then the purse is not unlike the sphere once imagined by Pascal to describe God—its diameter is everywhere and its center, nowhere; and we, its readers, are one of Martha Cerda's domestic creations.

Beyond Borges and Cervantes, numerous parallels come to mind, from Robert Coover and Georges Perec to Mary Poppins. But Martha Cerda is neither interested in minimalism per se nor in parodying popular culture, at least not visibly. Instead, she is obsessed by the leisure and fashions of the rich and sheltered in her native Mexico, a perfectly immobile class, self-possessed and egotistic, trapped in its own glorification. "One night," reads an early segment of the novel, "Señora Rodríguez dreamed that she opened her purse, and from it she herself came out, opening her purse; and from this one another Señora Rodríguez came out, opening her purse again; and so on." Her husband, on the other hand, "dreams that the purse is a bottomless well where what goes in never comes out."

He remembers the day when Señora Rodríguez
accidentally put her mother-in-law's picture inside
the purse and soon after that she died. And also when
by chance she put Señor Rodríguez's watch in the
same purse and Señor Rodríguez lost the notion of
time forever. That's why he gets up at three in the
morning to bathe and goes to sleep at five in the
afternoon, while Señora Rodríguez goes to the movies
and out for a cup of coffee with her friends and pulls
out the checkbook from her purse, caresses it and
puts it back, just like she put away the keys to her
house and even to the gates to heaven, so that no one
can enter without her consent.

Not Mary Poppins's umbrella but a checkbook and a watch: the purse is
a cosmic control panel and Señora Rodríguez, mighty and mysterious,
gently has the world at her mercy. She manipulates it at ease, without
ever realizing the fractured reality that surrounds her. Indeed, as the
reader flips this page and the next, we come to realize that Señora
Rodríguez's tentacles move in all directions. She wonders: Who am I?
Where do I come from? Nothing about modern Mexico matters to her:
not the unavoidable urban poverty, not the peasant insurrections, not
the governmental corruption. Not surprisingly, her serpentine replies to
her existential questions constantly point to her oligarchic roots in the
regime of Don Porfirio Díaz, a long-running dictator whose thirty-four-
year rule ignited the revolution of 1910 and who was accused by Mexican textbooks as the supreme benefactor and patriarch of a tiny elite. In
national slang any reference to his regime, *los tiempos de Don Porfirio,*
denotes a nostalgia for a period that was orderly and stable yet unreal,
and it is that period which Señora Rodríguez, refusing to acknowledge
the deterioration of civic manners around, desperately longs for. Similarly, the entire supporting cast—Señora Rodríguez's husband, their
children, Carlitos, Susanita, and the baby, Aunt Clotilde—to whom she
makes reference as she recognizes various items emerging from her purse,
are all snobs, symbols of a ruling class at once near-sighted and absent-
minded. So who am I? A rich lady lost in her purse. And what is Mexico?
Anything beyond this marvelous purse, of course.

Of all parallels and paragons, the most illuminating, the one that stands as perfect counterpoint to what Martha Cerda is attempting to do, is Italo Calvino, particularly in his very last novel, *Mister Palomar,* a meditation on routine published not long before his untimely death in 1985. Palomar (his name alludes to the famous observatory) does what we never expect a novelistic character to do: he goes shopping and to the zoo, looks at an ocean wave, reflects on his behavior in society, and even pretends to be dead; he is not part of an entertaining plot, nor does he serve as specimen to examine the rules of human conduct. Instead, Calvino turns the small volume devoted to him into a philosophical treatise, but one *á la mode*—unsystematic, open-ended, so heterogeneous that anything and everything can fit it, from a recipe to the whole yellow pages to the Bible. Cerda, wisely, takes Calvino's ploy a step further: she comments on Mexican politics by not alluding to them and turns Señora Rodríguez's elucubrations into sheer artificiality and melodrama. Had she, Señora Rodríguez, the opportunity of meeting Mr. Palomar, she would no doubt find him too cerebral, too systematic, for while his reflections are the result of the long European intellectual tradition, she, instead, has never been quite modern. Worse, she knows absolutely nothing about her national past, except, of course, for a few facts about Don Porfirio. A bit more entrepreneurial spirit and she could make a fortune selling her dreams of denial.

Cerda, born in 1945, in Guadalajara, Jalisco, is at the forefront of a miscellaneous troupe of inventive female literati from Mexico collectively devoted to the scrupulous inquiry of upper- and middle-class manners. (Other members of this troupe include Guadalupe Loaeza, Rosa Nissán, Sarah Sefchovich, and Angeles Mastretta.) This is her first book translated into English, and, from the three I have read, her best. Not to say that it is wholly successful. As the scene of Señora Rodríguez reaching into her purse is repeated, marginal tales are concocted, some involving her childhood, adolescence, and early motherhood, other pertaining to the novelist herself, and still a handful more ridiculing Mexican social habits. Several of these segments, while enchanting, at times seem written post-facto, as if Cerda, much like Walt Whitman and his *Leaves of Grass,* could not quite finish such open-ended work. But the postmodern ideal of this unfocused-focused novel works well even in spite of these segments. The novel is filled with anachronistic yet color-ful references to writers, local and international politicians, and natural disasters, to fairy tales and popular children's songs. Its most enduring contribution, I guess, is its indirect attempt at ridiculing the fancifulness of magical realism, a style that has done too much to disturb and rein-vent the Hispanic world. Who needs the Amazon jungle as scenario for the bizarre? It is in the minute and homey where the truly unexpected happens. Magic and exoticism are all buried in a lady's purse, and the purse itself is but a dream in the reader's mind. A purse full of junk, a continent full of dreams . . . or vice versa.

[1997]

SANDRA CISNEROS: FORM OVER CONTENT

Officially anointed *La Girlfriend* by the English-speaking media, Sandra Cisneros is considered a living classic. She is the most sought-
after Latina writer of her generation and a guest impossible to ignore in
any multicultural fiesta. The black-and-white photographs used to promote her work are colored by an overwhelming sense of theatricality.
They make her look like a sweet light-skinned Indian with a European
flair—a natural beauty out of a Sergei Eisenstein film. Her enigmatic
smile hides the ancient mysteries of her people, and her cowboy boots,
tiny miniskirts, idiosyncratic Mexican shawls, and hairbands inject the
needed exoticism into her ethnic roots.*

Her status as the voice of a minority has not befallen by accident.
Born in 1954 in a Chicago barrio and educated in the Midwest, Cisneros
acquired her distinct *tejano* identity when she settled in San Antonio in
the mid-eighties. She has since turned the U.S.–Mexican border into her
habitat. She proudly parades around under a hybrid façade, part nativ-
ist Spanish and part antiestablishment American. She is constantly ask-
ing her audience to approach her as the star of a cross-cultural
bildungsroman where *mestizas,* ignored and underrepresented for ages,
end up baking the cake and eating it all. Indeed, Cisneros describes herself as "nobody's wife and nobody's mother" and "an informal spokes-
woman for Latinos." Her imposed profile is that of an eternal sympathizer
of lost causes, a loose woman, a south-of-the-border feminist outlaw

---

* *I examine Sandra Cisneros in the context of Latin culture in* The Hispanic Condition
  (New York: HarperCollins, 1995).

happily infuriating anyone daring to obstruct her way. "They say I'm a bitch," a poem of hers reads,

> *Or witch. I've claimed*
> *the same and never winced.*
> *They say I'm a* macha, *hell on wheels,*
> viva-la-vulva, *fire and brimstone*
> *man-hating, devastating,*
> *boogey-woman lesbian.*
> *Not necessarily,*
> *but I like the compliment.*
>
> *By all accounts I am*
> *a danger to society.*
> *I'm Pancha Villa.*
> *I break laws*
> *upset the natural order,*
> *anguish the Pope and make fathers cry.*
> *I am beyond the jaw of law.*
> *I'm* la desperada, *most-wanted public enemy.*
> *My happy picture grinning from the wall.*

Her artistic talents are clear but overemphasized. In fact, what truly attracts readers is not her compact prose, which she perceives as "English with a Spanish sensibility," but her nasty, taboo-breaking attitude. Her works are pamphleteering. They denounce rather than move; they accuse rather than educate.

Responsible for several poetry collections, a children's book, and a couple of volumes of fiction, Cisneros hit high into the firmament with her 1984 novel *The House on Mango Street,* a chain of interrelated vignettes widely read from coast to coast and repeatedly assigned to undergraduates. The plot is unified by the voice of Esperanza Cordero, a preteenage girl coming to terms with her impoverished surroundings and her urge to write her life. Cisneros's second published book, with the imprint of Arte Público Press, a small nonprofit house at the University of Houston devoted to minority literature, *The House on Mango Street* came out just as she was celebrating her thirtieth birthday. The match between writer and publisher seemed ideal: a simple, cliché-filled coming-of-age tale by and about Hispanic women, uncomplicated and unapologetic, with the potential for enchanting a broad audience of young school girls, and a federally funded press whose mandate had been to place in bookshelves the fiction by Latinos that mainstream New York publishers refused to endorse. In a short time both parties benefited greatly, the unknown Cisneros becoming, without any major reviews, an incipient version of the *bandida latina* that would later blossom, and her title turning out to be one of the fastest selling in the house's catalogue.

That all happened when diversity and the politics of inclusion were still in diapers. By the late eighties, multiculturalism had become a national obsession, and a spokesfigure for the brewing Latino minority was urgently needed. Richard Rodriguez, whose autobiography *Hunger of Memory* had appeared in 1982, was already an illustrious presence, but his antibilingualism, often confused for anti-Hispanicism, seemed repugnant and xenophobic to the liberal establishment. Since Rodriguez stood alone, an unopposed male, a right-wing intellectual whose soul not even the devil could buy, a female counterpart was quickly sought. Cisneros seized the opportunity: Susan Bergholz, a Manhattan literary agent making a niche for emerging Latinos literati, took her as a client; soon after, Vintage agreed to reprint *The House on Mango Street* and Random House to publish another collection of stories, *Woman Hollering Creek*. A sudden metamorphosis occurred. Talented and outgoing as she was, Cisneros *la marginal* became Cisneros *la atractiva*. With the help of the right promotional machinery, she moved to center stage, and the applause hasn't stopped: from a Before Columbus American Book Award to a MacArthur Fellowship, she basks in the spotlight, sporting fancy sunglasses to reduce the glare.

But the problem, paraphrasing Gore Vidal, is that Cisneros wants to be not good but great, and so she is neither. Her style shows signs of maturity; her tales are not prepubescent anymore, and her sentimentality has mellowed down. *Woman Hollering Creek,* for instance, offers a gamut of pieces of self-discovery, set primarily in southern Texas and Mexico, often overstyled, on the role of women in our collective psyche: Rachel, narrating "Eleven," tells what it is like being a girl of that age; Ines Alfaro, who in "Eyes of Zapata" runs away with Mexican general Emiliano Zapata, talks about how his machismo destroyed her life;

Cleofila Enriqueta de Leon Hernandez, the character at the heart of the title story, follows her husband to the United States, where she realizes the extent of her own oppression—to cite only three among many other "suffering souls." These tales are neither fully original nor groundbreaking. Race and gender is their stuff, which Cisneros, by an act of cultural fiat, recycles with just the right ingredients to call attention to Hispanics as instinctual and exciting and interesting. For what they are worth, a handful are actually commendable, but the public has embraced them with far less ardor than it had *The House on Mango Street,* which isn't a good novel. It is sleek and sentimental, sterile and undemanding. Its seductive flavor, I guess, is to be found in its primitiveness. What Cisneros does is tackle important social issues from a peripheral, condescending angle, drawing her readers to the hardship her female characters experience but failing to offer an insightful examination of who they are and how they respond to their environment.

Since its republication by Vintage, *The House on Mango Street* has sold close to a quarter of a million copies. It might seem fine for seventh graders, but making it required reading in high schools and colleges from coast to coast, where students should have more substantial fare, is saddening. Its impact in the United States, obviously, has resonated worldwide. It has appeared in a dozen translations, including the unrefined Spanish one made by Elena Poniatowska, another one of Susan Bergholz's clients and Mexico's most important *femme de lettres.* Cisneros builds her narrative by means of minuscule literary snapshots, occasionally as short as half a page. Esperanza Cordero, whose name in Spanish means "hope," thinks aloud. She describes what she sees and hears in poetic terms, focusing on the women who surround her and the way they are victimized by men. The image of the house, a ubiquitous motif in so-called Third World fiction, becomes the central leitmotif: Esperanza's poor house embarrasses and pains her; she dreams of a larger, embellished one, a signature of the better times she yearns for for herself and her family. Men in her neighborhood are by nature evil; women, on the other hand, particularly the untraditional ones, are saintly, and she seeks a handful of them (Minerva, Alicia, Aunt Guadalupe) as role models. At one point Esperanza is raped as she accompanies her friend Sally to a carnival. At another, Sally is beaten by her father as punishment for seeing boys. The cast is presented as real folks but, in truth, it is Manichean and buffoonish. Together they introduce a risky rhetoric of virtue that utilizes the powerless victim to advance a critique of the Hispanic idiosyncrasy, but that fails to explore any other of its multiple facets.

Cisneros seasons her plot with the type of "magical realism" readers have grown accustomed to in Latin American masterpieces. This is done to make her work ethnic enough; it validates its authenticity. A witch woman, for instance, reads Esperanza's cards to unravel her destiny, and what she finds is "a home in the heart." Her identity quest is dissociated into alternative selves, all related to the various names she dreams of possessing. But her main concern is with the female body. Her descriptions of Esperanza's nascent sexuality are built upon the recognition of the opposite sex as a bestial monster ready to attack. A distant resemblance can be found between Cisneros's novel and Alice Walker's *The Color Purple*. Clearly Walker is much more concerned with relevant historical issues; she tackles slavery from a female perspective and reaches a level of high melodrama as her protagonist, Celie, undergoes a transformation from passive acceptance to self-assertion and human dignity. The epistolary structure of her book, as well as her use of dialect, give it a depth absent in Cisneros. Nonetheless, both writers resort to the same manipulative devices: their novels depict men within an ethnic minority as patently evil, and detail the psychological development of female characters who, only through conversion, can receive redemption. First you learn to understand the injustices of the environment, and then you become your own master.

Does the book deserve its current status? The answer is no. True enough, Latino fiction in English is still green, but turning *The House on Mango Street* into obligatory reading, presumably because of its accessibility, is wrong. It ratifies the image of Hispanics as sentimental dullards and, equally worrisome, it celebrates the Latino intellectual as pubescent protester. I do not mean to blame Cisneros for a wrong she is not responsible for. Hers is a first novel, a debutante's first turn around the dance floor. What is disturbing is the uncritical deification that surrounds her book. Scholars date the origins of the genre back to 1959, when José Antonio Villarreal published *Pocho*, a tale of revolution and assimilation, about a young Mexican-American kid facing discrimination and finding his rightful place in America. Since then a lot of what is published today by Latino fiction writers is realistic and semiautobiograph–

ical. The field is clearly awaiting a major breakthrough that will push its boundaries from conventional immigrant literature to a more sophisticated world-class writing, the type of transition carried on by Philip Roth and Saul Bellow in Jewish letters in the United States. Whenever such reformulating takes place, a recognition of earlier nontraditional voices will be crucial. Few, for instance, regard the pre-postmodern novelistic exercises by an Iberian, Felipe Alfau's *Locos: A Comedy of Gestures,* published in 1936, as a Latino ancestor, if anything because Alfau was a conservative fellow, unconcerned with ethnic envies, and also because, as a Spaniard, he automatically suits the profile of the oppressor. His novel, though, in the line of Pirandello and Italo Calvino, is light-years ahead of the immigrant-handles-it-all fiction we have grown accustomed to by a considerable segment of the Latino intelligentsia.

But the pantheon is vastly expanding, and high-caliber figures like Oscar Hijuelos, Julia Alvarez, Aristeo Brito, and Cristina García have already delivered commanding and mature novels, at once multifaceted and far-reaching, volumes that go far beyond easy stereotypes. Their understanding of what fiction ought to do—an investigation into the obscure aspects of humanity—makes Cisneros, by comparison, a far less demanding artist. Her messages come in soundbites and often have the taste of stale political sloganeering. She makes social protest the foundation for utopia. Trapped in her condition as Hispanic and woman, her creation, Esperanza, can only rely on her words and imagination to escape. She vows not to grow up tame, which makes her perceive poetry as the door out—her way of escape to an alternative life, her device to reject the ugliness of the outside world. So what type of literary model is *La Girlfriend?* Confrontational yet wholeheartedly anti-intellectual, her pen is just a weapon to incriminate. Nothing new in this, of course; after all, Cisneros is part, indirectly at least, of the illustrious genealogy of Latin American writers qua opponents to the system, from José Martí to Rosario Castellanos and Elena Poniatowska herself. But her ready-made U.S. odyssey, her "making it" in the American Dream, is curiously harmless. Hers is a domesticated form of belligerence. Rather than position herself as opponent to the powers that be, she courts them, feeds them with the dose of animosity they need, and in turn is fed lavishly by them on a diet of awards and prizes. Her forte lies in her articulation of words, not in her display and knowledge of ideas. She offers neither surprises nor profound explorations of the human spirit. The ethnocentrism that gives her legitimacy transforms her complaints into bourgeois manner-isms—transitory temper tantrums that society is ready to accept simply because they present no real subversive threat. Her tales are flat and un-original and thrive on revising moribund stereotypes.

In short, the acclaim granted by the liberal establishment to *The House on Mango Street,* and to this nineties version of the flamboyant Mexican artist Frida Kahlo, as the classic Latina writer of her generation, is, to me at least, a form of collective nearsightedness and one more evidence of how exoticism pays its dues. What forces us to give simplistic, overly accessible novels, fiction cum caricature, to the young? Are they allergic to more complex readings? Or could it be that our research into the archives of Latino literature has not gone far enough? By endorsing Cisneros's attitude and no one else's, the risk of falsifying the role of Latino intellectuals is quite high. All serious literature, by definition, is subversive, but in our MTV age, not all of its needs to be foul-mouthed and light-weight.

[1996]

Tina Modotti, *El machete,* 1927. Courtesy of the Museo Nacional de Arte, Mexico City.

TINÍSIMA

*T*inísma is many books in one: a voluminous novel about the notorious Italian photographer and activist Tina Modotti (1896–1942); a travelogue; a photo album; an annotated collection of Modotti's correspondence; and a catalogue of the innumerable personalities she came across during her stints as a Communist in France, Spain, the Soviet Union and the Americas both north and south of the Rio Grande. That Elena Poniatowska, Mexico's foremost *femme de lettres,* almost succeeds in annealing these elements into a smoothly tempered whole is testament to her huge talent as a fiction writer and amateur historian.

Poniatowska's objective is not to scrutinize Modotti's heavy-handed Stalinism or correct center-right intellectuals like Octavio Paz, who have all but dismissed her photographic legacy. The novelist is after something altogether different: apprehending the inner life of a suffering woman obsessed with rebellion, both on the street and in the privacy of her bed. Modotti wasn't a prolific photographer, and neither was she a very original one. Her images, compared with those of Lola and Manuel Álvarez Bravo, the foremost Mexican photographers of her era, or with those of her teacher and lover Edward Weston, are tame and superficial. But they are unsettling: Modotti thrived in exploring the status quo and used her lens to express anger at the social iniquity she witnessed. She became a *cause célèbre* and today is ranked with Henri Cartier-Bresson, Eliot Porter, Paul Strand and Weston as among the most imaginative foreigners ever to photograph Mexico. She might not have been the most genuine of artists, but her explosiveness paid off.

This only partly explains why Poniatowska and other contemporary Mexican intellectuals are fascinated by Modotti. Since the early eighties, she has been the subject of a spate of essays, retrospectives, plays, films, and television documentaries in Mexico. Her status is now not unlike that of Frida Kahlo—a kind of south-of-the-border equivalent of Camille Claudel. Both Kahlo and Modotti have been turned into postmodern heroines who belong to *les années folles,* the romantic period that extended from the twenties to World War II and served as a stage on which female idealists sacrificed everything—their bodies, their souls, their talents—to endorse macho causes. They were women who loved their men too much (Weston, Diego Rivera, Auguste Rodin) and ended up paying a heavy price. They also perceived themselves as the eclipsed half of the relationship, even when they were both sun and moon to their male lovers. The difference between Kahlo and Modotti, of course, is that Kahlo made an art of exhibiting her own suffering. Modotti's photographs are only occasionally autobiographical, and she rarely turned the camera on herself. Furthermore, Modotti's art seems secondary to her political odyssey, in which she was used, abused, and even turned into a scapegoat by friends, government, and press. Modotti has all the attributes of martyrdom—and martyrs, after all, embody a sense of sacrifice and loss. In this respect, the recent renaissance can be seen as the nostalgia of contemporary Mexican intellectuals for a time when the intelligent urban left truly mattered.

Poniatowska starts with Modotti's most scandalous year, 1929. Julio Antonio Mella, her lover, an exiled Cuban activist, is assassinated on the streets of Mexico's capital, and as he lies dying on the pavement he accuses the dictator Gerardo Machado of plotting his end. It is an unstable epoch for the nation and a dangerous season for foreign militants. Armed insurrections have taken place not long beforehand, and Álvaro Obregón, running for a second chance as president, has been killed by a fanatic. As a war is openly declared against Communists, seen as traitors and antinationalists, the Partido Nacional Revolucionario, the forerunner of today's ruling Partido Revolucionario Institucional, is founded.

In this atmosphere, Modotti, well known for her licentious sexuality and for her radical politics, is accused of complicity in Mella's death. The Mexican press, in particular the powerful daily *Excélsior,* makes her case look like a preview to O. J. Simpson's: Excerpts from police interrogations are published regularly, as are photographs real and concocted, interviews true and imagined, and other forms of yellow journalism. Modotti is quickly turned into a symbol. As loyalists counterattack the government-sponsored campaign against her, she takes refuge in Tehuantepec, but soon after, in 1930, is publicly accused yet again, this time of plotting against the newly elected president, Pascual Ortiz Rubio. She is convicted, and after a brief stint in prison is asked to leave the country immediately. Thus ends Modotti's most artistically productive and politically vociferous period.

Thus, also, begins the most enthralling sections of *Tinísima*. About a third of the book is set in Europe and the Soviet Union, where Modotti lived after her departure from Mexico. Poniatowska plaits in her early life as well, from her period as an actress in Hollywood (in 1920 she was cast in *The Tiger's Coat,* directed by Roy Clements) to her affair with Weston, in whose studio she studied in Los Angeles. After a lack of commitment on both parts, the couple moved together to Mexico City, settling at 42 Veracruz Avenue, on the corner of Tampico, a house-turned-shrine where, as I write, an enlargement of Weston's famous 1924 photograph of Modotti's bare-breasted torso hangs to commemorate the hundredth anniversary of her birth. The pathos of her story, though, lies in her late Mexican days, as she shakes hands with luminaries who changed the nation and the world. Although Poniatowska doesn't waste energy injecting this section with a unique narrative cadence, to readers interested in the crossroads of art and ideology in the Hispanic orbit, and particularly the muralist era in Mexico, this portion of the novel is stellar.

Poniatowska's research is estimable: Modotti's liaison with the Mexican Communist Party and her collaborations in its organ, *El Machete*; her friendship and subsequent confrontations with José Clemente Orozco, Rivera, and Kahlo; her multiple and multifaceted lovers, native and foreign; and her links to other left-wing Latin Americans and to Marxist groups in France, Germany, Italy, and Spain are littered with cameo appearances of all sorts, proving that Mexico between wars was the ultimate meeting ground of dreamers. At one point D. H. Lawrence passes by, and so do Jean Charlot, Augusto César Sandino, Vladimir Mayakovsky, B. Traven, Sergei Eisenstein and the Peruvian José Carlos Mariátegui. This parade ends with Pablo Neruda's eulogy to Modotti, the first stanza of which reads:

Tina Modotti, sister, you do not sleep, no,
you do not sleep,
Perhaps your heart hears the rose of
yesterday
growing, the last rose of yesterday, the
new rose.
Rest gently, sister.

If the abundance of references seems often overwhelming (novel and index usually preclude each other, but I vote in favor of attaching one to a future edition of *Tinísima*), it hints at the method by which Poniatowska composed her book. Highly regarded in what has come to be known as *literatura testimonial,* a genre perfectly suited to the Hispanic reality in that it gives voice to the voiceless, she is responsible for the classic *Massacre in Mexico,* a pastiche of news clippings, poems, photographs, transcriptions of interviews, and other paraphernalia about the 1968 government-sponsored slaughter of hundreds of students in the Plaza de las Tres Culturas, in Tlatelolco Square, Mexico City. The technique of cut-and-paste is also apparent in her prolific journalism, published in the newspaper *La Jornada,* as well as in her miscellaneous book of anecdotes and news reports on the 1985 earthquake in Mexico's capital.

Poniatowska's fiction is almost always historical, its characters drawn to resemble closely their real-life counterparts (as in *Dear Diego,* an epistolary fiction about Angelina Beloff, Diego Rivera's first wife). Facts are presented as such—Poniatowska's interest lies not in blurring genre distinctions but in using the novel as a means through which to rehumanize our view of legendary characters and explore their vulnerabilities. Her most remarkable work of fiction has not appeared in English translation. Titled *Hasta no verte, Jesús mío,* it is an exploration of early twentieth-century Mexico from the eyes of a stolid lower-class woman of admirable character—a counterpoint to *Tinísima* in that the two visit the same period from opposite ends of the social spectrum.

Modotti's letters, her photographs which open most chapters, the frequent quotes on top of quotes, the news reports—these make for a demanding revisionist read. If Poniatowska can be a master of polyphonic documentaries that are funny and moving, she can also be wordy and repetitious, and this book showcases both extremes. The plot is poignant and its presentation insightful but also challenging in its redundancies. Given Poniatowska's proclivity to overemphasize, to accumulate data, to turn narrative into archive, however, the good news is that the English translation by Katherine Silver may be seen as something of an expurgation. After all, the 1992 Spanish original ran to 663 pages. Something was gained in translation: The basic plot remains but unfolds with fewer obstacles.

The novel is a welcome addition to what is already becoming a trend: volumes of fiction and nonfiction from Mexico attempting to limn the labyrinthine paths of the nation's ever-disoriented left. The results are mixed: Some, like the thrillers of Paco Ignacio Taibo II, particularly those with his private eye, Héctor Belascoarán Shayne, as protagonist, are at once parodic and consciously derivative; others, such as *The Mexican Shock* by Jorge Castañeda, or *A New Time for Mexico* by Carlos Fuentes, are impressionistic studies, some more personal, others more scholarly, attempting to understand the present challenge and intellectual roots of figures like Cuauhtémoc Cárdenas and Subcomandante Marcos. Poniatowska's *Tinísima* stands alone among them. It focuses on the most daunting period of Mexican left-wing utopianism, is ambitious in scope, and places full attention, for a change, on the feminine. The picture of Tina Modotti that emerges is that of a romantic protofeminist misunderstood and abhorred by the macho society around her, a woman whose camera mattered far less—to her and her contemporaries—than her tragic fall from grace. It is a telling picture, one that says much about Mexico's turbulent past, and about its nostalgic present.

[1996]

FILMS

Like Water for Chocolate

An occasional screenwriter and a one-book-only novelist, forty-two-year-old Laura Esquivel is one of Mexico's most popular writers. Beyond all expectations, *Like Water for Chocolate,* a best seller published there in 1989, has sold close to a million copies in Spain and in the vast Hispanic America and has been translated into numerous languages, including English. (The U.S. edition was brought out last fall by Doubleday, translated by Carol and Thomas Christensen.) Set on a ranch on the U.S.–Mexican border, not far from Piedras Negras and San Antonio, this romance with highbrow overtones explores the Rio Grande as an abyss where Anglo and Hispanic cultures collide, a no-man's-land of hybrid idiosyncrasy. Plotted from the late nineteenth century to a climax during the rebellious years of the socialist revolution of Emiliano Zapata, the book has a crystalline feminine flavor. Recipes for Mexican delicacies like quail in rose-petal sauce, northern-style chorizo, and beans with chile Tezcucana-style are offered at the beginning of each of the twelve chapters, with home remedies for ailments also intertwined. And the intellectual and spiritual weight of Esquivel's six protagonists—Tita, Mama Elena, Nacha, Rosaura, Gertrudis, and Chencha—authoritarian and well-to-do matrons, opinionated young girls, *soldaderas,* and maids, serves to map the trajectory of feminist history in Mexican society; machismo is the book's hidden object of ridicule.

Part of *Like Water for Chocolate* was written in New York, where the author lived with her husband, Alfonso Arau, a Mexican actor who has worked in Hollywood (he appeared in Sam Peckinpah's *The Wild Bunch* and Alejandro Jodorowsky's cult film *El Topo,* as well as in *Romancing the Stone*). Arau is also the experimental director responsible for south-of-the-border hits like *Mojado Power,* a satire of the Chicano movement of the late sixties; *Calzonzin Inspector,* based on a comic-strip character; and *The Barefoot Eagle,* about an unlikely Mexican superhero. Given the novel's remarkable commercial success (there were more than 202,000 copies in print in the U.S. at last count), Esquivel and Arau joined forces in adapting it for film (she is given the credit for the screenplay, he produced and directed). The result is not only of high quality but ought to be seen in larger scope as the return of Mexican cinema to the international market of film festivals and first-run art houses.

During the forties and beyond, the so-called Golden Age personified by Emilio "El Indio" Fernández, Gabriel Figueroa, and Fernando de Fuentes, Mexican films received worldwide applause and were incredibly influential. *María Candelaria* and *Los Olvidados* were awarded top prizes at Cannes and elsewhere, and Pedro Infante, María Félix, Jorge Negrete, and Mario Moreno, the Hispanic Charlie Chaplin known as Cantinflas (who died just a few weeks ago), were ubiquitous in the Caribbean, Spain, and Central and South America. It was the age of the Good Neighbor Policy, and this filmic notoriety sustained itself for a couple of decades, only to evaporate. A deteriorated film industry reached its nadir during the scandal-plagued presidential regime of José López Portillo, when it was deprived of any significant government financial support; it was finally declared dead in March 1982, with the explosion and subsequent demolition of the Cineteca Nacional, Mexico City's legendary film archive and museum on Tlalpan Avenue.

The slow and painful agony coincided with the wide impact of Hollywood comedies and blockbusters that descended over the nation's theaters, a phenomenon that managed to fully alienate the audience from its own country's film resources. In the seventies, almost the only productions made in Mexico were grade-B movies about prostitutes, drugs, and violence, with sex symbols Isela Vega, Sasha Montenegro, Jorge Rivero, and Valentín Trujillo in titles like *The Hustlers* and *Rape.* (Frequently these were destined for an eighteen-to-twenty-four-year-old male audience living in East L.A.; innocent of artistic pretensions, they are a banquet for scholars interested in popular culture. Although less than mediocre in quality, these films mirror the collective psyche. Women are untrustworthy whores and deserting wives, while men always need to display their overweening force and courage.) The industry also found itself competing against soap operas produced by the private television network, Televisa, owned by the tycoon Emilio Azcárraga, which represent a favorite middle-class pastime. Until very recently hopes of recovery seemed slim.

But miracles occur. Critics today are talking with due optimism about a renaissance of Mexican film. Not only have we witnessed the emergence of a handful of extraordinary young directors like Maria Novaro, Guillermo del Toro, and Dana Rotberg but also the resurrection of veterans like Gabriel Retes, Jaime Humberto Hermosillo, and Arturo Ripstein. Examples include *Danzón,* María Novaro's second feature, an impressive 1990 lyrical narrative with actress María Rojo in the leading role, and *Red Sunrise,* also with Rojo (who, by the way, manages to be part of the cast in virtually every important renaissance film). *Danzón* is about a lower-class telephone company worker and dance aficionado who, after the loss of her partner, travels to Veracruz to find him in what becomes a voyage to unravel her own feminine identity. The film has won international acclaim and was released in the United States last year. *Red Sunrise* exhibits a clear Eastern European style and is about the 1968 Tlatelolco Square student massacre, as seen from the interior of an apartment building. Besides these titles, dozens of others with screenplays by respected Mexican writers are booked in Mexico's theaters, where a new audience eagerly awaits them; they frequently win distribution overseas as well.

The recipient of ten Ariel Awards of the Mexican Academy of Cinematographic Arts and Sciences, as well as a number of prizes in the Chicago, Tokyo, and Toronto film festivals, *Like Water for Chocolate* (the expression is used in Mexico to describe a state of sexual arousal), in its unraveling of the novel's convoluted sentimentality, is at the forefront of this renaissance. Most of the action takes place in the ranch kitchen, where Tita, the twenty-four-year-old strong-willed third daughter of Mama Elena, condemned to a life of impossible love, enjoys cooking delicacies for her family and friends, the town's priests, and any passersby. Traces of magic realism, a style usually attached to Latin American literature but unquestionably present in Brazil's *cinema novo* and in the art of the Argentine director Eliseo Subiela and other auteurs from the region, is everywhere: When Tita is ready to take revenge against her mother, a sister, and a boyfriend, she prepares a powerful *mole* that upsets everybody's stomach; when she is sad, her dishes make people cry; and if she is passionately in love, her sensual recipes ignite lust in her many guests. Unpretentious and honest, the film is Mexico's response to *Babette's Feast*—a display of food as the cook's weapon and an investigation of what Italo Calvino, in *Under the Jaguar Sun,* called "the Mexican way of taste."

Acting may have been one of the handicaps of Mexican cinema during the seventies, but the surprising performances of Lumi Cavazos (Tita) and Regina Torné (Mamá Elena) in *Like Water for Chocolate* are neither parochial nor underdeveloped; they are tours de force that leave the viewer hungry for more. The set design by Emilio and Ricardo Mendoza and Gonzalo Ceja authentically reproduces the style of the U.S.–Mexican border at the turn of the century and is extraordinary when compared with the numerous disasters made since Ripstein's *The Holy Office.* As a director, Arau uses (at time abuses) close-ups to give a sense of intimacy and domestic pathos.

To be sure, his film is no masterpiece. The soundtrack is miserable, and the fact that it used non–Spanish-speaking actors like Marco Leonardi (*Cinema Paradiso*), who needed to be dubbed, has embarrassing consequences. Still, *Like Water for Chocolate* is infinitely better than the average product that emerged from Mexico after the Golden Age faded. And yet, good news in Mexico is often transitory. This welcomed renaissance is a result, in part, of efforts by the Instituto Mexicano de Cinematografía (IMCINE), headed by Ignacio Durán Loera. This government agency is devoted to promoting and developing original screenplays, to funding co-productions on the premise that film is not necessarily a money-making industry but is an essential element in the country's culture. Since its resurrection in 1988, when Carlos Salinas de Gortari began his six-year presidential regime, IMCINE has been offering incentives to attract investors and has opened doors that coordinate the technical and creative processes. Although soap operas still invade most Mexican living rooms every weekday, a genuine enthusiasm toward Mexican films is felt across the social spectrum. But a presidential election is scheduled for next year, and the candidate's philosophies could well determine whether Mexican cinema continues its ascent or begins another period of decline. Meanwhile, *Like Water for Chocolate* provides an expression of a new Mexico, one enchanted with the drama and lyricism of its daily images, ready to seize the moment to use movies as a tool to explore the collective self.

[1993]

Like a Bride

Guita Schyfter is a pioneer in that her films (two up until now) are invariably devoted to exploring a facet of Mexico seldom addressed by others: the uneasiness, the discomfort with which the country has welcomed its immigrants. While the nation's population is made of disparate ethnic and racial ingredients—part European, part aboriginal, but neither one nor the other—minority groups, after two or three generations, always fail to assimilate, to find themselves fully at home. They end up constructing an insular collective identity based on difference; and while they shine and prosper, they build their ghettoized life on the fringes of society, as if they were Mexican only by sheer accident.

That, indeed, is the central theme of *Like a Bride,* to my knowledge the first movie ever to examine the introversion and anxiety of Mexican Jews. But it is pioneering in other aspects as well: this, after all, is the first Latin American film partially spoken in both Ladino and Yiddish; and it is also the first one to include scenes about the impact of Zionism on young left-wing Jews and to ponder the presence of the *Shomer Ha-Tzair* in Mexico. Those of us who grew up in and around downtown Mexico City, in the Narvarte and La Condesa neighborhoods, are overwhelmed by the shock of recognition: until now these scenarios of our childhood and adolescence were secluded in the dark chambers of memory. But the director has metamorphosed them; she has transported them to the big screen and thus introduced them as part of the global domain.

Schyfter, then, is an eye-opener. Through their individual clashes with their respective families and with the gentile milieu, her two heroines are like trapeze artists walking on a fragile cord: no matter where they are, they always find themselves on alien turf, strangers in a strange land. They must define themselves not by who they are but by what is ex-

Still from *Like a Bride*. Archivo del Instituto Mexicano
de Cinematografía. Reproduced courtesy of the Cineteca
Nacional, Mexico City.

pected of them. And since they belong to very different linguistic and
traditional backgrounds (one is Ashkenazi, the other Sephardic), their
dreams and expectations take them on different paths. Based on an autobiographical novel by Rosa Nissán and with a screenplay largely shaped
by the playwright Hugo Hiriart, Schyfter's film honestly examines the
fractured structure of the Mexican Jewish community, the tension that
has prevailed since the early forties, splitting its 50,000-some members
into small ethnic fractions seldom seen together.

Not surprisingly, the response to *Like a Bride* by the community el-
ders has been nothing but lukewarm: after its original release in 1993,
they expressed fear that its negative portrait of the constituency would
promote anti-Semitism in the nation as a whole and increase tension

among community members. A typical response, one should say: from Spinoza to Philip Roth, every time a courageous Jewish artist ventures into a potentially explosive domain, she or he is met with silence. Happily, Mexican critics and audiences fell in love with the film's content and appreciated Schyfter's openness. My own guess is that they reacted in such a way because the movie is not only about Mexico's response to immigrants, but about being Mexico in general.

[1994]

A Kiss to This Land

Was it Sigmund Freud who said that to be a Jew is to be in the opposition, eternally antagonistic, a unity against all pluralities? Little of that antagonism can be deduced from Daniel Goldberg's film, the first documentary feature of its kind to reflect on the Mexican Jewish experience. Its focus is the early immigrant generation, the founding fathers and mothers, mainly from Eastern Europe, responsible for establishing the *yishuv*—opening a *kehila*, building libraries, synagogues, and philanthropic organizations, distributing newspapers, establishing Hebrew and Yiddish schools.

I still wonder how they managed to replace *mujiks* with *manachis*. They had left their memories behind and were beginning anew in the lands of Cuauthjémoc and Benito Juárez. And they were blessed: they prospered and quickly rose in the social hierarchy, their patriotism evident in what one of Goldberg's interviewees calls "our kiss to this land." But Mexico for them was never a Promised Land: they had arrived on its shores by chance, when quotas in the United States shut the doors to their dreams, and their sense of belonging to a country where slavery and the Holy Inquisition had been abolished not too long before was fragile at best. Obviously they couldn't afford to fool themselves: *Amerika* symbolized prosperity, freedom, leisure—the "authentic" New World; Mexico, on the other hand, was a theater of corruption and social upheaval not unlike the one they had left behind.

No, Mexico was not America. In spite of its warm welcome, the country was obviously not at ease with itself. Jews, even those of Sephardic

Publicity photo from *A Kiss to This Land*. Archivo
del Instituto Mexicano de Cinematografía. Reproduced courtesy of the Cineteca Nacional, Mexico
City.

ancestry, would constantly be perceived as the devil's friends—abusive,
untrustworthy, treacherous. Subsequent Jewish generations would have
a more troubled love for the country: some would eventually leave, making *aliyah* or moving to Florida. A tiny fraction would assimilate, but
the majority would find ways to accommodate to a ghettoized atmosphere, remaining distant and uninvolved in national affairs. The result

Poster of *A Kiss to This Land*. Archivo Cineteca
Nacional. Reproduced courtesy of the Cineteca
Nacional, Mexico City.

is tangible. If Goldberg's immigrants felt grateful, their children, and even their children's children, would nourish an ambivalence toward Mexico, slowly becoming "the opposition"—an insular minority.

A number of questions emerge from *A Kiss to This Land*: What, for instance, has been the ongoing response by the Jewish community to anti-Semitism in Mexico, sponsored by the Church and often endorsed by the government? How is it that Yiddish remains a spoken language when elsewhere in the world it is almost defunct? What, if any, is the role of Jews in Mexico's cultural realm and in its diplomatic circles? And what to say of the Jewish membership in Communist parties? Obviously Goldberg didn't set out to address all of these issues, but his inquisitiveness raises issues that ought to be explored and that, in some way, are becoming the subject of films on second- and third-generation Mexican Jews, like Guita Schyfter's *Like a Bride*. When the full history of the community is written, it will become clear how its constituency lived between two geographic poles: on this side, American Jews, egomaniacal and self-centered; on the other, Baron de Hirsh's Argentine settlers, a solid community of *pamperos*. It will also show how decade after decade, Mexican Jews remained incredibly proficient in the ways of tradition, even though that tradition changed dramatically from one generation to the next. And I am confident that that history will also explain how, once Goldberg's immigrants passed away, their followers would feel uneasy about kissing the land.

[1995]

Strawberry and Chocolate

This film, the latest offering from Cuban director Tomás Gutiérrez Alea (Titón), has won popular and critical acclaim on a scale unprecedented for Cuba's film industry. It netted an award at Robert Redford's Sundance Film Festival, an Oscar nomination for Best Foreign Film, and widespread distribution from both Redford and Mirimax Films. But while the film is an impressive breakthrough for Cuban cinema, it is also, in less obvious ways, a bittersweet farewell to the tradition of Cuban revolutionary cinema—a movement Titón helped found in the sixties—as well as a pained and largely unresolved meditation on issues of sexual identity under Castro's notoriously repressive policing of the Cuban gay community.

The film is also important in that it speaks to Titón's recent experience as an exile from Castro's Cuba: His recent bout with cancer forced him to leave the island before the movie's completion, leaving the movie in the hands of Juan Carlos Cabio, a young, irreverent Cuban filmmaker. Titón traveled to the United States for treatment, and now that his health problems have somewhat abated, he has become a Spanish citizen and is working on two new films. Titón's return to Europe—as a young man, he studied film at Italy's Centro Sperimentale—is being greeted as treason by his former compatriots in Cuba and as a triumph of personal will by the Cuban exile community. But both responses reduce his departure to a political act, ignoring its creative dimensions. To judge by *Strawberry and Chocolate*—especially in the context of Titón's earlier work—the director's exile comes not a moment too soon, at a time when he is wrapping up his major artistic obsessions. Tempted to conceive of freedom in different terms—to perceive the Iron Curtain from the other side—Titón has broken with his formal, cinematic past, even as many of his thematic concerns remain unchanged.

In an interview some twenty years ago, Titón was asked about the advantages he saw in working under a state-owned film production system like Cuba's. Such working conditions were challenging but also incredibly rewarding, he replied. "I imagine that is a very difficult thing for the majority of people living in a nonsocialist country to understand," he added. "They find the idea of giving up certain limited bourgeois freedoms to be a very painful one because they are unable to conceive of freedom in any other terms. For me, their point of view has very grave limitations." He went on to explain that artists under communism in Cuba enjoy much greater freedom because they are "in control of what they are doing," whereas under capitalism, the "system based on unequal exercise of power and influence *always* works in the favor of the most powerful."

And yet the Cuban system has always posed grave limitations of its own for Titón's work—notably, limited funding and state censorship that have conspired to make the time between his completed projects very long. Hiatuses of five years and longer have separated one film from the next. Still, ever since his first feature, a documentary-style work on the miserable conditions of mine laborers called *The Charcoal Worker* (done in collaboration with Julio García Espinosa), Titón has always remained loyal to unraveling the enigmas of Cuba.

One of his classic works, *Memories of Underdevelopment*, nicely drew out his ambivalence about the role of the artist in Cuba by including, near its end, a celebrated TV speech Castro delivered at the dawn of the Cuban missile crisis. "No one is going to come to inspect our country," Castro pronounced, "because we grant no one the right. We will never renounce the sovereign prerogative that within our frontiers we will make all the decisions, and we are the only ones who will inspect anything." Along with the other artists of Cuban revolutionary cinema, Titón took Castro, somewhat courageously, at his word—proceeding to understand Cuba from within, and then examining its contradictions from a more universal standpoint. In the process, he analyzed the role of the nation's intelligentsia and studied, in cinematic terms, Cuba's ethnic and ideological background. All of Titón's films—from the historical work *The Last Supper,* which explores the tension between Christianity and Afro-Cuban religion, to light comedies such as *Letters from the Park* (based on a Gabriel García Márquez story)—delineate the island's struggle with its own conflicted cultural identity and the revolutionary excesses of the Castro regime.

Strawberry and Chocolate brings these same themes to bear on the issue of homosexuality, loosening and abandoning many of the conventions of Cuban revolutionary cinema along the way. Titón's new film parodies romantic Hollywood styles and subverts gender stereotypes to create a cast of Cuban characters at once brave and introspective, all quintessential Westerners deeply rooted in Cuba's hybrid cultural tradition.

The film sets out to re-evaluate Cuban machismo, approaching questions of sexual identity and gender differences bravely, free of inherited taboos. Its appearance has more or less coincided with the international uproar surrounding the autobiography of the late gay émigré writer Reinaldo Arenas. Arenas's book *Before Night Falls* contends, among other things, that at least two-thirds of Cuban men have had a gay experience but will do anything to deny it. And Arenas is only the most visible member of a growing community of Cuban homosexual artists. Others, like writers José Lezama Lima, Severo Sarduy, Virgilio Piñera, and Senel Paz, have suffered persecution under Castro's repressive policies toward gays. Paz wrote the original story and screenplay for *Strawberry and Chocolate.*

Compared to Arenas's memoir of the severe repression and repeated torture he suffered in Cuba because of his sexual preference, Titón's film is tame. While Titón does address the atmosphere of intolerance, prejudice, and bigotry that surrounds Diego, the film's gay protagonist, he includes no scenes of terror or physical violence. Nonetheless, like Arenas's book, *Strawberry and Chocolate* generated a huge controversy both within Cuba and beyond. Some sources in Cuba have claimed that the Castro regime's initial response was simply to withhold the film from both domestic and international distribution. But a resistance movement soon began, and government censors changed their minds: The movie was widely screened in Cuba and endorsed as the nation's entry for the Oscars. The regime's reversal was more than a little calculated— its acceptance of Titón's timid rendering of gay repression is a cheap way to quiet the gathering uproar over more militant statements like Arenas's.

Gay groups abroad, particularly throughout the Hispanic world, have denounced the regime's about-face. They contend that Havana has acted hypocritically, endorsing a comparatively light treatment of the plight of Cuban gays while still subjecting them to widespread harassment and sending them to concentration camps to "reform" themselves. The distribution of Titón's film, they argue, creates the false impression that *glasnost* is under way for Cuban gays.

While the film itself may not usher in a new age of tolerance, it does shed some valuable light on some of the tensions—both personal and political—of gay life under Castro. Jorge Perugurría plays Diego, a sweet and flamboyant gay man, a dilettante with a baroque apartment in downtown Havana. Thanks to Perugurría's candid, compassionate performance, Diego is the movie's main attraction.

The plot, however, revolves around David (Vladimir Cruz), a younger man, apparently straight, whom we meet in the movie's first scene—a sexual liaison with his girlfriend that he is unable to consummate. In the next scene, she gets married to another man, and David finds himself alone, wandering around a park. At this point he encounters Diego, who starts courting him. Their bumpy association provides the core of the film's thematic agenda—an exposé of the falsities and incongruencies of Cuban communism. In spite of his loyalties to justice and equality, Diego, the film implies, will always be perceived as undesirable, an unacceptable element in society. He will be ridiculed and tormented so that others can find solace in their so-called normality.

The other central character is Nancy, a prostitute and amateur *santera* played by Mirta Ibarra, Titón's wife in real life. She is Diego's neighbor, counselor, and close friend, offering him advice in his pursuit of young David. Soon, however, Nancy discovers she is also attracted to David, and a rivalry between her and Diego unfolds. This plot twist offers Titón the opportunity to shape Diego as the film's unquestionable hero and the voice of Cuba's conscience—a role he fills bravely and ebulliently. At one point, Diego characterizes Castro as "Cuba's only voice" and describes the nation's culture under him as saddening and desolate. His courtship of David proves abortive: Diego is forced to leave the country—but not before he invites Nancy to fulfill his own hopes of initiating David into the pleasures of sex.

In spite of the film's courageous engagement with the issues of gay identity under Castro, the overall mood of *Strawberry and Chocolate* is gentle to the point of virtual harmlessness. While the political denunciations in the film are welcome, they strike the viewer as flat and limited. Titón is only ready to go so far. It's a hesitancy that prevents personal expressions of gay sexuality from being anything more than harmless, as well. Unlike Héctor Babenco's *Kiss of the Spider Woman,* in which the gay and straight protagonists seal their intimacy with a kiss, *Strawberry and Chocolate* climaxes with a hug—at once a sign of departure and a nonthreatening affirmation of gay male sexuality. And the plot's resolution of the crisis in David's sexual identity comes across as innocuous and naive.

But for all its many imperfections, *Strawberry and Chocolate* is endearing. As a farewell to Cuban revolutionary cinema, it successfully evokes the great demons against which Titón once fought. And in one sense, it remains true to the revolutionary aesthetic: It subverts and questions Cuba's own archetypes of masculinity and sexuality by turning its protagonists into fragile creatures ready to defy old certainties. It is, in many ways, a fitting point of departure for the director's new dilemma of exile. Cuba, no doubt, will remain the heart of his work, but his new vantage on it will pose a considerable challenge. José Martí once talked of two Cubas: one on the island and the other outside. Will they finally prove to be one and the same? Titón might have the answer.*

[1995]

* *Tomás Gutiérrez Alea died on April 16, 1996.*

LAURA ESQUIVEL'S SECOND ACT

Laura Esquivel's best-selling first novel, *Like Water for Chocolate,* released in Spanish in 1990, not only holds the enviable distinction of having reinvented a whole literary subgenre—the recipe novel—but, almost as important, is single-handedly credited, in the orbit of Latin American fiction, for carrying on a torch that Manuel Puig left unattended after his premature death, at the age of fifty-seven: the torch of melodrama. Set in a hacienda on the U.S.-Mexican border during the peasant revolution of 1910, the book is about a domineering mother and her three daughters, particularly the youngest and most rebellious one of them. But it is also about true love as an unstoppable, all-conquering force, about a domesticated type of feminism, and about the mystical side of womanhood. Esquivel's international success had two immediate results: it quickly turned her into an easy target of envy, and it elevated her to the status of indisputable queen of Hispanic melodrama. While more than three million readers worldwide fell under her spell in at least thirty languages, few if any critics could collect enough strength to call it a work of art. Instead, from Rome to Tel-Aviv, from Montevideo to Tokyo the book was described as "overinflated," "manipulative," "farfetched and cartoonish," all attributes of melodrama, an esthetic form not displayed in full scope since Puig's legendary *Kiss of the Spider Woman* appeared in 1976. Some critics even accused Esquivel of simplifying the lives of Mexican women. It is true, but what is melodrama if not a simplification? For the form to work, one needs to do precisely that—overinflate and manipulate human emotions *ad infinitum.*

Intriguingly, in progressive circles Esquivel has actually been turned into some king of a New Age guru. She is regularly featured in alternative magazines, where she talks about the human side of technology, as well as about ecology and transmigration of souls. This might sound anachronistic for those linking success with egocentrism, but Esquivel, in spite of her overwhelming celebrity, seems to keep herself afloat by retaining a spiritual side. This can be explained, in part, by her middle-class Mexican background. Indeed, she belongs to a generation of women that came of age in the seventies, hypnotized by Orientalism, angered by the repressive atmosphere of the PRI regime, and mesmerized by the 1968 student massacre in Tlatelolco Square. The insurmountable pollution superpopulation in the Mexican capital triggered in Esquivel's age group a fever for Jungian philosophy and for the type of mystical experiences made popular by Carlos Castaneda in *The Teachings of Don Juan*. The result was a kind of esoterism linking the end of our millennium to the end of the world, explaining history as a struggle between opposing energy fields, and endorsing a kind of transtemporal view of the nation itself in which the Aztec past and the postindustrial future are deeply connected.

Numerous Mexican novels, comic strips, TV soaps, and radio serials dwell on this trend, as does Esquivel's second novel, *The Law of Love*, now available in English in Margaret Sayers Peden's translation. It is in this book that her New Age side emerges most clearly. A masquerade of epic proportions, it begins in the 1523 conquest of Tenochtitlán, the Aztec center known today as Mexico City, as Rodrigo, a Spanish knight married to Isabel, is raping Citlali, an Indian beauty. The scene is filled with astonishing cruelty: sex and love are intertwined, and when the mix proves too unbearable, Rodrigo kills both Citlali and her newborn child. Never fear: the fatal attraction is meant to continue up until the twenty-third century, as the souls of the passionate lovers transmigrate toward their ultimate redemption. As the plot unravels Citlali becomes Azucena, an "astroanalyst," a sort of highly advanced therapist capable of searching for her Twin Half across time and space. And indeed, Azucena will hunt Rodrigo through 14,000 past lives and, in the process, unravel a macabre plot by a fraudulent reincarnation of Mother Teresa who uses her false identity to become President of the Planet.

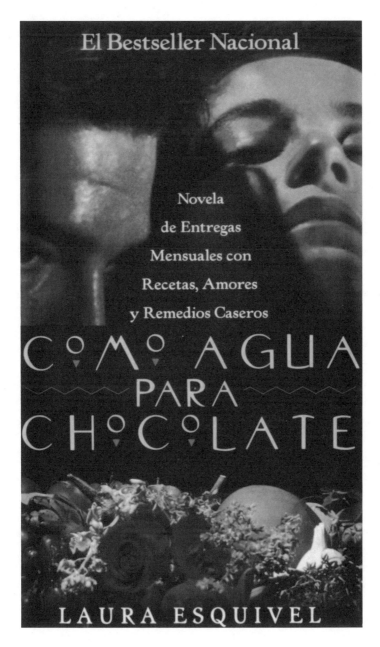

Cover of *Como Agua para Chocolate*, Anchor Books
edition, 1992.

Implausible? Too far-fetched? Esquivel seems to have gone amok . . . but wait, there is more to it. Unhappy with what the novel as a literary genre can offer, Esquivel accompanies it with a variety of media accessories. *The Law of Love* is not only filled with quotes from pre-Colombian Nahuatl poems, it also comes complete with a CD that features major hits from Puccini operas, such as *O Mio Bambino Caro* and *Nessum Dorma,* all of which are intertwined with Caribbean and Mexican rhythms, like *Burundanga* and *San Miguel Arcángel.* The reader is asked to turn on the stereo when a certain character is in a lousy mood, or else, when a soul is undergoing a cosmic metamorphosis. Simultaneously, Esquivel has invited the Spanish cartoonist Miguelanxo Prado to illustrate certain passages of the plot in which one of the protagonists is having a vision or *déjà vu.* These full-color illustrations are not in the form of cartoons adding to what the text says, but self-sufficient graphic passages that both the characters and reader can visualize without the need for words. The only comparison I can think of is John Berger's *Ways of Seeing,* which alternates critical and visual essays on modern art. In the latter ones, a set of famous images parade in front of the reader's eyes without a single word to unravel their meaning. We alone must come to our own conclusions.

All this explains why Crown is promoting it as "the first multimedia novel." Innovation, obviously, is the key word: Esquivel has taken both her novelistic talents and her guru status to the limit. The problem is not in the concept but in its execution. As in *Like Water for Chocolate,* the prose in *The Law of Love* is flat and unremarkable, except that in this case the plot is so convoluted, so ridiculous, the reader longs for some sort of relief. To describe Rodrigo's divided loyalty to Citlali and Isabel, for instance, Esquivel goes for the most infantile of approaches: "He had to divide his body in two separate Rodrigos," she writes. "Each fought for control of his heart, which would completely change according to which of the sides was winning." Her futuristic scenes are mere gags to discuss a certain utopian technological device. And the whole transmigration reverie is approached as a "recyclable process," without anything particularly refreshing about it.

Before turning into a celebrity, Esquivel was a shadowy screenwriter and the wife of Hollywood actor and director Alfonso Arau. She embarked with him on an adaptation of *Like Water for Chocolate,* and the collaboration left an immense profit when the film swept the Ariel Awards, the Oscar equivalent in Mexico, and went on to become the largest grossing foreign movie ever released in the United States. But success is a sour affair: half a decade later, Esquivel and Arau are not only divorced but their lawyers are in the midst of a huge legal battle in which he is accused of embezzlement; and she has, at least until recently, moved to Manhattan, where anonymity is perhaps a bit more tangible than south of the Rio Grande.

Trashing Esquivel has become a sport, and I am guilty of it. Will her second novel become a best-seller? Judging by the volatile excitement in Spain and Latin America, I have serious doubts. The book was published with much fanfare but the hoopla quickly evaporated. For a better product, we might need to wait for Esquivel to show up in a better reincarnation.

[1996]

BORDERLAND: A LETTER*

Dear Alfred:

Your letter was awaiting me as I returned from a week-long lecture trip to El Salvador. What better moment to reflect on the nature of borders than after a journey to a region where not long ago rifles were the law of the land? As you well know, during the sixties Latin America was perceived as a fertile ground to construct millenarian utopias. But hope has turned sour and nowadays the only utopia is based on the emulation of the age-old enemy—the United States. Poverty reigns in El Salvador, the Frente Farabundo Martí para la Liberación Nacional has become an ineffectual political force, and more than 2 million Salvadorans, almost half the national population, live in voluntary exile north of the Rio Grande. This mammoth exile is prompting people to ask, Where does the country begin and where does it end?

El Salvador, of course, is not alone in its plight to redefine its collective identity. We all are. In a world increasingly run as a transnational corporation, migration and translingualism have become a pattern.

---

* *This text was written at the invitation of Alfred MacAdam, editor-in-chief of* Review: Latin American Literature and Arts, *for the special section of issue 54 that gathered twenty-six statements by Latin American and Latino writers and artists on the subject of the frontier, concrete and abstract, in this fin de siècle.*

Decades ago José Vasconcelos envisioned *el mestizaje,* the mixing of ethnic and racial groups, as a pattern for the future. His prophetic teachings ought to be seen as a sequel to those of W. E. B. DuBois in that, if the problem of the twentieth century has been the problem of the color line and the relation of the darker to the lighter, the next century will no doubt be about hybridization and miscegenation, about fusing colors and tongues.

I myself was born in Mexico into a Jewish family of Russian and Polish descent. Yiddish was almost as important in my education as Spanish, and Hebrew followed closely behind. All of which made me *different.* And since difference is frightening to adolescents, my answer to the identity question some fifteen years ago was Marxism: I fought against difference and dreamed of homogenization. Clearly, a foolish dream, for you know me well, Alfred: I look anything but Mexican; in fact, I can easily pass for a Wasp. Realizing that appearance *is* fate, I decided, much like the many Salvadorans in transit to *El Norte,* that I would settle in the United States and in 1994 became a naturalized citizen. Today I live a bilingual, bicultural, and binational life, constantly traveling back and forth to *el Distrito Federal* and beyond, from Cantinflas to Chaplin and back. You know, in El Salvador people today can't help using the past tense to describe their present; in the United States, on the other hand, it is the future that counts. But no language—neither Spanish nor English—is truly my own. Likewise, both Latin America and the United States make me feel like an alien resident. Only my accent, I guess, which at this point is untraceable to most people, feels unique.

Perhaps all this is what being Jewish is about. For what is a Jew if not a time-traveler, a creature lost and found in translation, a citizen just like everyone else—except a little different? I am not at all sure what we, the Chosen People, were chosen for, but I have no doubt that that selection (or better, *segregation*) process pushed us to become the *rara avis* we are. Identity is an enjoyable labyrinth with no exit.

Television channels in El Salvador are filled with dubbed American programs. I watched them totally mesmerized. I grew up watching shows like *Star Trek, Colombo,* and *Lost in Space,* where American actors had Mexican accents, and so there wasn't anything new for me. But somehow I had forgotten about this ubiquitous translating feature in my native home and to see it again made me revisit the way in which televised mouths move at one speed and their imposed voices at another, usually slower one. To me this retardation, this gap between movement and word, is what separates one culture from another. And that is the only border that concerns me personally. Geographical borders are by nature artificial. Foreign languages can be learned. But the abyss between one idiosyncrasy and another is inexorable.

I hope all is well with Barbara and the kids. Let's talk soon . . . in Spanish.

[1997]

BUFFALO NICKEL

We have witnessed a boom of Latino fiction in English in the past few years. Unlike its earlier avatar from south of the Rio Grande, which catapulted to international stardom a handful of "Third World," Spanish-speaking, male novelists and acquired its most tantalizing success in *One Hundred Years of Solitude,* this literary awakening is by Latinos—that is, Mexicans, Puerto Ricans, Cubans, Dominicans stationed for decades in the United States—who, curiously, need now to be translated back into their original tongue to be read by their relatives. Multiculturalists are applauding: At last this most troubled ethnic minority is stamping its own signature on the pages of American letters.

In retrospect, 1990 may come to be seen as a signal date for this revival: the year Oscar Hijuelos won the Pulitzer Prize with *The Mambo Kings Play Songs of Love,* a best-selling tale about Caribbean music, lust, and brotherhood in the New York City of the forties. Other titles by Latinos had been nominated before for national awards, but this one caught the eye of a literary establishment suffering from attention deficit. Suddenly, major trade publishing houses began to recognize the commercial value of Latinos and rushed to sign new books. A plethora of novels and short-story collections materialized in a short period; while some were disappointments, others, notably by Sandra Cisneros and Julia Alvarez and Cristina Garcia (women are among the leaders in this boom), were quite impressive. To be sure, for years many of these writers had been loyal to small, university-based presses like Arte Publico in Texas and Bilingual in Arizona. But a handsome advance and the possibilities of enviable exposure became magnets for those interested in making it big. The phenomenon equals the awakening of a general audience in the United States to Jewish novelists like Philip Roth and Bernard Malamud in the sixties and blacks like Toni Morrison and Alice Walker in the seventies. Today, of course, these four are no longer "minority" voices— they are national treasures.

I use the word *revival* to describe the phenomenon because a common mistake is made when appraising the freshness of this new wave. The fact is that whatever is reaching us today is the result of a slow process of maturation and empowerment, a voyage from the periphery to the center of culture, from marginality to acknowledgment. *Locos: A Comedy of Gestures,* for instance, a masterpiece by Felipe Alfau, a Spaniard living in the United States who is considered today a precursor of postmodernism alongside Borges and Pirandello, was published in 1936. Later came José Antonio Villarreal's 1959 novel *Pocho,* considered the first Chicano novel written in English. The parade continued with John Rechy (aka John Francisco Rechy-Flores), whose *City of Night* was an instant success in 1963; Piri Thomas's *Down These Mean Streets,* a 1967 memoir about Puerto Ricans in Spanish Harlem; Oscar "Zeta" Acosta's *The Revolt of the Cockroach People,* detailing the plight of Chicanos during the civil rights era, written a half dozen years later; Rudolfo Anaya's prize-winning *Bless Me, Ultima,* which has sold more than 300,000 copies; Rolando Hinojosa's *Sketches of the Valley and Other Works,* which began his renowned Klail City Death Trip series; and Edward Rivera's *Family Installments,* another autobiographical account by a Puerto Rican about the difficult personal transition from the Caribbean to New York, which appeared in the early eighties. (The inclusion of Cuban writers to the canon comes as a late addition, simply because the 1959 revolution that forced many into exile did not generate fluent English-speaking fiction writers until some fifteen years later. Today, besides Hijuelos and Garcia, Pablo Medina and Elías Miguel Muñoz have published outstanding books.) Now that a more benign, receptive intellectual climate has begun to flourish, literary historians have a treat at their disposal: the opportunity to trace stylistic roots and analyze the politics of acculturation in a long-standing tradition.

When considering the impact of this new boom, a crucial question is how its readership is shaped. If for decades the English-speaking Hispanic novelist was solely the property of academic circles and a small elite of authors' acquaintances, the entrance to the commercial stage implies another sort of audience. Victor Villaseñor and Sandra Cisneros, for example, are now not only widely read but are part of the college curriculum in Florida and the Southwest and are slowly being similarly recognized in New England. One ought not to forget that fiction by Latinos written in Spanish—brought out by Mexican, South American, or Spanish publishing houses—is also an essential, although still unrecognized, part of our cultural landscape. As a Latino, to choose English as a literary vehicle is to live with a self divided as badly as Jekyll and Hyde.

Among the precursors of the current Latino literary boom in the United States is Floyd Salas, a novelist and boxing coach. Born in 1931 in Walsenburg, Colorado, he is the author of *Tattoo the Wicked Cross* and *What Now My Love,* two novels published in 1967 and 1970. The protagonist of the first is a hard-core *pachuco,* not unlike those discussed by Octavio Paz in *The Labyrinth of Solitude,* whose sense of identity and enchanting innocence will be lost forever after prison, where he is tortured and raped; the image of an insecure fellow in a violent underworld recurs in the second title. After an enthusiastic critical reception, Salas was perceived as a promising talent. In 1978 he published a third novel about the uprising at San Francisco State University in the sixties, *Lay My Body on the Line,* but then vanished into literary oblivion. His disappearance exemplifies the odyssey of Latino writers at large, at least until 1990. After a stunning debut often comes neglect: Alfau, to return to the same examples, took over forty years to publish his second novel; Villarreal is practically hidden from the public eye; and Thomas is now completely ignored. One, of course, hopes the present climate of enthusiasm for works by Latinos will be a prolonged one.

What did Salas write while eclipsed? A handful of screenplays and two historical novels, one about the Yankee conquest of California in 1847 told from the point of view of two members of the Spanish aristocracy; another set in 1806, also in California, about the romance between the Russian czar's high chamberlain and the daughter of a Spanish commandante. But in spite of his early success, nobody would print them.

In his youth, Salas was arrested five times for brawling and served 120 days in Santa Rita Prison Farm for spitting in a cab driver's face. Awarded a boxing scholarship (the first of its kind) at the University of California, Berkeley, he has never been shy about expressing his opinions. In

1968, for instance, he challenged Saul Bellow personally by attacking his views of the university as a haven of vulgarity. (The incident appears in Bellow's *Mr. Sammler's Planet.*) Salas's newest book, *Buffalo Nickel,* a coming-of-age memoir about a troublesome urban adolescent who is a passionate boxer, is a showcase of his triumphs and defeats, an exposé of his world view and ideological stand, a sideboard of the best and worst in him. It might not be the author's best, but at least it manages to reinstate his name in the current literary constellation.

At center stage are Salas's two older brothers: the boxing champ Albert, whose early success leads to drug addiction and a life of crime and irresponsibility; and Edward, a bisexual in the Marines who as an intellectual prodigy is awarded a scholarship at Harvard University Medical School and is upwardly mobile enough to open his own pharmacy in San Francisco. This *bildungsroman* of sorts takes place in the underworld of Oakland, full of pimp bars, steamy whorehouses, and suffocating prisons. Floyd Salas himself, torn between his two brothers, seems like a visitor from outer space lost on earth. He oscillates between Al, who personifies confusion and perdition, and Eddy, a symbol of enlightenment and the possibility of happiness. His ultimate allegiance—body or intellect? glove or book?—is not entirely unpredictable.

Attacking the art of Joyce and Faulkner, Isaac Bashevis Singer once claimed novels should concentrate on actions and not on thoughts. When you read the newspaper, he said, you never find what someone was thinking but always his deeds. Salas doesn't waste a single word on a character's internal meditations. *Buffalo Nickel,* originally called *Brother's Keepers,* a name discharged for its proximity to the title of a memoir by John Edgar Wideman—emerges as an honest, deeply felt journalistic account of struggle in the urban battlefield, a shocking portrait of inner-city life and death. Poverty, toxic saturation, and illiteracy are problems reflected upon in great detail to study the voyage an individual undergoes from drug addict to messiah of rehabilitation.

The volume's major drawback is found in its structure: While the first half is engaging and melodic, the second is a sum of precipitated ends, as if Salas had to rush in order to make the entire story fit fewer than 350 pages. A case in point: Although the death of the protagonist's mother is described patiently and persuasively, as the memoir progresses, a number of Al's children commit suicide at such a fast pace that the reader runs out of compassion and breath. Also, crucial epoch-making scenes in Salas's life are narrated with such a high degree of melodrama that the book at times seems imitative of the afternoon soaps.

Yet, autobiography is a favorite literary genre for recording personal struggle, and Salas's book might be seen in contrast with such notable memoirs by Latinos as Thomas's *Down These Mean Streets,* Acosta's *The Autobiography of a Brown Buffalo,* and Richard Rodriguez's *Hunger of Memory.* His urge is to tell of his pilgrimage in novelistic terms without excesses, in a conventional, linear fashion; he targets his story for the reader ready to find inspiration in this type of odyssey.

Shortcomings aside, *Buffalo Nickel* deserves attention. The fact that this hardcover is published by Arte Publico demonstrates how vital a role small presses still play in the current literary boom of English-speaking Hispanics. Salas's art, complete with its naturalistic overtones, seems a good weathervane from which to learn much about today's Latino writers—to understand where this ethnic minority comes from and what occupies its present intellectual endeavors. The Latinos writing in the United States are younger, on average, than were the pillars of the Latin American boom when they achieved prominence here, which to me suggests very good things to come. When some of the new "ethnic" voices become national treasures themselves, it will be in part because the generation of Salas, Anaya, Thomas, and Hinojosa served as their compass.

[1993]

APPEAL OF THE FALSE *QUIXOTE*

The identity of Alonso Fernández de Avellaneda, author of *El ingenioso hidalgo Don Quijote de la Mancha,* still unavailable in English after almost four centuries, remains a puzzle. He has been the subject of intense debate and heated speculation. Only five clues of his evasive biography have reached us so far: that he was born and died between the seventeenth and eighteenth centuries, although exact dates are missing; that he was a friend or acquaintance of Lope de Vega, a hugely successful playwright during Spain's Golden Age; that he was a devoted Christian; that he published, in 1614, under Felipe Roberto de Terragona's imprint, his only book, known today as *The False Quixote,* which contains the Third Adventure of the most memorable Spanish novelistic couple, the so-called Knight of the Saddened Figure and his useful servant, Sancho Panza; and that his name was a mere pseudonym behind which the Aragón inquisitor Alonso Fernández could be hidden, or perhaps the Dominican friar Mateo Luján de Saavedra, also known as the creator of an apocryphal sequel to another Iberian classic, *Guzmán de Alfarache.* A hunger for more clues persists.

We've somehow gotten used in this end of the millennium to literary sequels: to Mitchell's *Gone with the Wind,* to Bronte's *Wuthering Heights,* to Austen's *Pride and Prejudice,* to Tolstoy's *War and Peace.* Sherlock Holmes and Emma Bovary began as creations of a single, original writer, and then turned into money-making machines in the hands of less-inspired plagiarists. That's essentially why Avellaneda continues to fascinate me: He inaugurated a most distinguished tradition, the art of turning literature into kitsch, a tradition taken to astonishing heights particularly in Latin America, where, by definition, everything modern is a by-product, a hand-me-down.* By doing so, he was among the first to link originality with plagiarism, genius with mediocrity, purity with filth. What persuaded him to falsify Cervante's oeuvre? Surely the huge success of *Don Quixote de la Mancha,* Part I, published in 1605, and the impatient delay for Part II, which would not reach its readership until a decade later. Some critics have also ventured the possible animosity between the two writers, who surely knew each other. Their intertextual dialogue is quite haunting: Avellaneda states in his Prologue that Cervantes "went out of his way to offend me"; and Cervantes, portrayed in *The False Quixote* as a despicable type "to whom everything and everybody makes him angry, who lacks any true friends, and whose best literary fortunes are the *Galatea* and not his novels but his prose comedies, neither satirical nor exemplary," constantly ridicules Avellaneda in *Don Quixote of La Mancha,* Part II.

What this means, of course, is that both literary works are eternally linked, regardless of the little attention given to Avellaneda outside Spain and Spanish. I, for one, have always kept them together in my private library. Since I was very young, I have kept Avellaneda's spiritless work next to the many editions and translations of Cervantes, among them one illustrated by Gustave Doré. Prepared by the scholar Marcelino Menendez y Pelayo, my edition of *The False Quixote* was published in Barcelona in 1905 by the Librería Científico-Literaria de Toledano López, Cía. I bought it in an antique bookstore in downtown Mexico City. Similarly, my favorite English translation of the real *Don Quixote,* by Tobias Smollett, was given to me by an Israeli lover sometime around 1980, not before inscribing its title page with the following moralistic epigraph by Bertolt Brecht: "Some men fight a single day and are good. . . . But others struggle an entire life and are irreplaceable."

Leopoldo Lugones, Jorge Luis Borges, and Paul Groussac have argued, and rightly so, that Miguel de Cervantes Saavedra, a one-handed soldier born in Alacalá de Heneres in 1547 and dead in 1616, was a poor stylist but an inspired fabulist. His descriptions are often boring, his sentences

---

* See my essay *"Translation and Identity,"* in Art and Anger *(Albuquerque: University of New Mexico Press, 1996), pp. 187–203.*

and paragraphs repetitive and labyrinthine, but his Hidalgo and Sancho Panza remain eternal archetypes because their creator injected them with an astonishing, unparalleled dose of universality. Avellaneda, on the other hand, had absolutely no sense of language or plot and is even less remarkable as a dreamer. His pages are full of syntactic chaos and uninspired malapropisms, and his unredeemed Quixote is far less ingenious, less affecting than Cervantes's. And yet, unifying authenticity and falsehood, production and reproduction, glory and ignominy, intonation and derivativeness, literature as art and literature as merchandise, the two *Quixotes,* clearly, are one and the same. The fact that we are fully acquainted with Cervantes's true identity and not with Avellaneda's is, in my mind, a sign of the kind of partial, incomplete, single-faceted respect we grant human genius.

[1992]

ROSARIO FERRÉ'S MACONDO

There is a border in contemporary Puerto Rican letters that is at once mental abyss and tangible geographical gap between island and mainland, one that literature can map in astonishing detail. Remarkable books like *La noche oscura del Niño Avilés,* an intriguing, encyclopedic 1984 novel by Edgardo Rodríguez Juliá about religious fanaticism, set in the eighteenth century in San Juan Bautista, remains unknown and untranslated this side of the water. And like Juliá's, plenty of original fiction goes unappreciated abroad. Similarly, the work of classic English-language Puerto Rican writers like Judith Ortíz-Cofer, Edward Rivera, and Piri Thomas is underrepresented on their Caribbean island of origin. A dialogue of silences, no doubt, which Rosario Ferré has intelligently managed to solve by splitting herself and her audience in two. She is a perfect embodiment of the Janus-like identity of Puerto Rican literature today, faces set back to back, impossibly "loyal to two fatherlands," as the memorialist Bernardo Vega once put it.

Born in Ponce in 1938 and educated at Manhattanville College and the University of Maryland, where she received her Ph.D., Ferré is first and foremost a Latin American *femme de lettres*—baroque, portentous, savvy, erudite. This might sound odd in light of her latest novel, *The House on the Lagoon,* a family saga of epic proportions about European immigrants and mulatto servants, which she wrote in English. (In 1989, *Sweet Diamond Dust* proved Ferré adroit at self-translation, as did her subsequent English rendition of much of *The Youngest Doll,* a collection of her stories.) Yet such literary bilingualism, too, can be read as emblematic of her island's disjointed soul, and it follows that each of her audiences will have a different set of expectations and tastes.

Up until the nineties, Ferré's career unfolded mainly among a Spanish audience, but her strategy is obviously changing. Her artistic breadth, emotional ardor, and intellectual appetite, it seems to me, are direct descendants of the boom generation in Latin America. Like her colleagues Luisa Valenzuela and Cristina Peri Rossi, she was influenced by the improvisational cadence of Julio Cortázar, about whom she wrote a critical study. Over a span of twenty years, Ferré has produced many volumes of fiction, poetry, retellings of Puerto Rican legends and folk tales, literary criticism, and feminist scholarship.

Ferré is the daughter of Luis A. Ferré, a self-made Puerto Rican millionaire and one-time governor with the capital in, among other places, the cement industry and a media emporium that includes Puerto Rico's leading newspaper, *El Nuevo Día*. Her family tree is obviously one inspiration behind her new novels, which is almost candidly autobiographical in a way American readers should find lively and enlightening. Like most wealthy households in Puerto Rico today, Ferré's includes a wide range of opposing political views, from *independentismo* and statehood to support of the island's status as a commonwealth, from an open endorsement of Spanish as the official language to the relentless fight to make English the national tongue. That multiplicity of clashing viewpoints is the engine behind her book. Her objective, it seems, is to deliver a grand chronicle of Puerto Rico's political and emotional upheavals in the twentieth century by juxtaposing the diplomatic and cultural spheres with the domestic sphere. The result is sweet, if occasionally flaccid.

One problem with the approach is that although Ferré has labored to make her protagonists three-dimensional, the reader cannot but sense an almost operatic texture, with love, hate, and tears staged at every turn. Political views are presented in tabloid black and white, and clichés are not uncommon, as in the following.

> Quintín and Isabel would never see eye to eye politically. Quintín was for statehood and liked to think of the United States as his real country. He considered himself not a citizen of Puerto Rico but an American citizen—a citizen of the world. "If Puerto Rico ever becomes an independent nation, like the Nationalists and Independentistas would like," Quintín would tell Isabel, "we'll be

on the first plane to Boston, where my family still owns some real estate."

Quintín considered Nationalists and Independentistas a dangerous lot. Nationalism was more a faith than a political conviction, and Nationalists were fanatical.

Her prose simple and unadorned, Ferré *la barroca* has been replaced here by Ferré *la accesible*, a writer mimicking early forms of realism à la Balzac and Zola. The structure is straightforward, verging on predictable. Some stereotypes of Puerto Ricans—debated by many, including the illustrious playwright René Marqués—are put to rest, at least partially. Ferré's characters, women and men alike, are possessed by destructive demons forcing them to eliminate any obstacle impeding their success. In fact, Ferré's creatures, while characteristically Hispanic, have features straight from traditional American immigrant sagas: humble, self-motivated, expatriate male dreamers in search of fortune; well-to-do wives parading at benefit galas, keeping secret lovers, and nurturing artistic drives.

The plot moves forward harmoniously, with fiction playing out the forces of history as tropes. This book will evoke thoughts of other family chronicles, some sober, some exaggerated and overemotional, from Isaac Bashevis Singer's *The Family Moskat* to Carol Shield's *The Stone Diaries*, from Tolstoy to Salman Rushdie—multigenerational adventures that Mario Vargas Llosa once described as "total novels" about . . . well, in Ferré's case about everything viewers of Univisión and Telemundo might expect.

But Ferré's novel is seasoned not so much with rivalry and ideological radicalism as with prophecy, *santería* sorcery, and Afro-Caribbean witchcraft. And that, I'm afraid, is where the main weakness is to be found. Her narrative suffers from what I shall call "the Macondo syndrome," a condition through which writers seem bent on replicating *One Hundred Years of Solitude*. Her novel's resourceful design, its structure, its pathos are derivative of Gabriel García Márquez, to the point of annoyance. Or better, they seem to be modeled after imitations, such as Isabel Allende's *The House of the Spirits*. *The House on the Lagoon* features a novel within a novel, much like the scrolls of the Gypsy Melquíades. Although individual protagonists trace their roots to Spain and Italy, the plot officially begins in 1917, when Buenaventura Mendizabal, the narrator's father-in-law and the family patriarch (reminiscent of the founder of García Márquez's Buendía dynasty), disembarks from the Virgen de Covadonga in Puerto Rico. And it ends with a plebiscite in contemporary times, when fictional *independentistas* stage a takeover, kidnapping an important executive.

The cast of hundreds includes Isabel Monfort, the heroine and talented narrator, a bit of a recluse not unlike Rebeca, the Buendías' adopted daughter. Then there's Milan Pavel, an architect from Czechoslovakia and Frank Lloyd Wright's protégé, known as "the Wizard from Prague," who resembles Pietro Crespi, the suicidal Italian music master in García Márquez's classic. And, finally, at the heart of Ferré's volume is Petra, a clairvoyant mulatto maid, like Pilar Ternera, the generous woman of easy virtue frequently sought out by the inhabitants of Macondo.

Resemblances, imitations mirroring other imitations, characters possessed by the strange feeling of being unoriginal, simple echoes, residuals, hand-me-downs are of course what contemporary Latin American letters are all about. Evidently, Ferré is capable of mastering the recipe. Unfortunately, she doesn't dare take it a step further, subverting its mechanisms. It's a pity, at least for those readers with any form of literary memory.

Yet with *House on the Lagoon,* Ferré consolidates her niche in a growing tradition of Latin American novelists, represented by, among others, María Luisa Bombal and Manuel Puig, capable not only of translating themselves but of creating original fictional universes in the English language. She also brings to a wider audience, in charming fashion, the dilemmas of Puerto Rico's divided self, painfully torn between two loyalties since the Spanish American War, if not since earlier colonial times. It remains to be seen if the reception to her book breaks the pattern of oblivion granted so many Puerto Rican works published in the United States. (One positive sign is that it was chosen as a finalist for this year's National Book Award.) Somehow, the Anglo milieu, in its provincialism, has not embraced the *oeuvres* of Eugenio María de Hostos, Luis Pales Matos, José Luis González, Ana Lydia Vega, and other islanders, and to a lesser extent that of Puerto Rican mainland writers.

[1995]

AUTUMN OF THE MATRIARCH

Carlos Fuentes once rather pompously referred to Luisa Valenzuela as "the heiress of Latin American fiction" who "wears an opulent, baroque crown, but her feet are naked." That was in the early eighties, when her dislike of dogmas and certainties, her explorations of the uses of ambiguity, her forays into "that reflective field where reality appears at its most real" were the constant subjects of features, book reviews, and heavy literary commentary, a time when she could reign unchallenged as the best-known and most-translated contemporary woman writer of the Southern Hemisphere. But things have changed dramatically since then. The region's literature is in crisis today, with luminaries like Valenzuela seemingly unable to find a way out of their artistic quagmire.

Other eloquent female voices have entered the scene on a grand scale, signaling a variety of alternative styles and themes. Instead of shying away from the kitchen and its gastronomic potentials, and rather than evading melodrama and sentimentality in their work, they have delved into those realms wholeheartedly. The result is a type of women's writing that is commercially successful on levels never experienced by Valenzuela, and that subverts by way of consorting with and exploiting the status quo. This sort of literary renewal is evident not only among women but also among young, curious writers of both sexes who are devoted to experiments with subgenres like thrillers, science fiction, and romance (Luis Supúlveda's ecological whodunits spring to mind, for example).

One of the causes precipitating a sense of the doldrums in Latin American fiction is the everlasting compulsion to make politics a *sine qua non* in fiction. The tentacles of tyrannies have been everywhere in the Southern Hemisphere for centuries, and naturally the writer's voice has come to symbolize resistance and rebellion. Valenzuela, who has spent almost as much of her adult life in her native country, Argentina, as she has abroad in Europe and the United States, believes the primary purpose of literature is to disturb, to agitate—not by repeating trite political slogans but by questioning our perception of reality. Since her debut in 1966, her literary project has carried on the legacy of astute playfulness of her compatriot and unquestionable tutor, Julio Cortázar, the author of *Hopscotch* and *Blow Up,* who died suddenly in 1984. Cortázar's second creative period, from the moment he identified with Fidel Castro's revolution on, was marked by critical barbs aimed at repression and taboos. Less inventive but equally shrewd, Valenzuela roams the same themes and displays similar stylistic pyrotechnics. She enjoys walking the tightrope between religious fanaticism and heresy, deciphering the macabre link between torture and pleasure, and reflecting on the heavy weight of collective history. Even when her topic is sex and superstition, as in her most celebrated novel, *The Lizard's Tail,* its implications are invariably intertwined with politics, cruelty, and death. The subject of that 1983 book was José López Rega, the controversial minister of social welfare and personal secretary to Isabel Perón. Rega, a self-proclaimed astrologer who helped rule Argentina through sorcery, had a curious physical abnormality: three testicles. Valenzuela investigated his fanciful life, delivering a demanding, lucidly self-conscious political novel that constantly challenged the reader's expectations. To revolt, then, has been her lifelong activity. She opposed tyrannical regimes, machismo, bourgeois society, and traditional writing styles.

At a time when to accuse meant to unsettle, to unnerve, Valenzuela's much-needed message was quite popular. As the Argentine military junta propagated a dirty war against alternative forces, writers like her became magnets of international attention, and efforts to silence their voices proved ineffective. But now dictatorship has given way to democracy, even if tenuous, throughout Latin America with the exception of Cuba, and the transition to civilian life is proving to be a mammoth challenge to old-guard literati like her. As in Jean-Paul Sartre's theory that Jews need anti-Semites to exist, once Perón, Stroessner, and Pinochet left the spotlight, "oppositional" writers have suddenly found themselves with a limited audience, their prose turned morose, infirm, unappealing. Dissension, as everybody knows, is good literary business.

Valenzuela's youthful bravura has mellowed. Her sharp revolutionary edge seems not tepid but mismatched to current realities, and the role of articulating Argentina's passage to democracy has evaded her. As exemplified by *Bedside Manners*, her latest and probably most evanescent novel to appear in English (originally published in 1990), nostalgia and depression, permanent features of the Argentine psyche, have become somewhat pervasive in her development. The autobiographical plot pertains to a female writer's attempt to understand the drastic, chaotic changes affecting her country since the military regime gave up power. Almost immediately upon her arrival home after a decade-long exile in New York, the *Señora*, as the protagonist is addressed, accepts an invitation from a new friend to spend time alone in a bungalow at a local country club in an unnamed city (presumably Buenos Aires), where she is to recover and assimilate the heterogeneous stimuli now bombarding her. Her friend tells her: "The club isn't one of those flashy places, it might not seem much to someone like you coming from abroad, but it's actually very private and exclusive. They don't let just anyone in."

She packs a bag with the bare essentials—white sheets, a white nightgown, and an empty notebook—and sets off for the "unknown but singularly unthreatening destination." All too soon she finds out that the club is located next to a training camp where extreme-right military forces are planning a coup d'état. As the narrative progresses, TV images, one of Valenzuela's favorite motifs, become ubiquitous and are indistinguishable from reality. Visions keep flying out of the TV set, confusing the *Señora* even more. Strange encounters and flirtations begin to occur with an eccentric cast of characters, portrayed as vultures and hyenas ready to extort and abuse her. She is first visited by an obnoxiously idiosyncratic maid, María, who keeps turning the TV on and, ironically, while trying to pull her out of depression, never stops repeating that the nation's currency is worthless and inflation is under such fast rhythm that the currency is already lighter than air. Then comes Doctor Alfredi, ready to take sexual advantage of her while diagnosing her melancholic status; Lucho, a miserable, insubordinate soldier often found under the *Señora's* bed; and the patriotic Major Vento, who justi-fies his hyperkinetic military actions in the camp by claiming that the country is plagued with dangerous looters and left-wing agitators who profit from the difficulty social situation, and who thinks the army should demoralize and disrupt daily life in order "to crush the malcontents."

The novel has a distinctive Beckett-like atmosphere; its narrative oc-casionally switches from first to third person and utilizes phrasings that simultaneously employ both philosophical and matter-of-fact dimen-sions. Yet it also reminds me of Anita Brookner's *Hotel du Lac*, in which a woman looks for relaxation in a country home only to find inner per-plexity. Valenzuela's entire adventure takes place within the boundaries of the bungalow, where the air is increasingly suffocating, sleep is insuf-ficient, and the public and domestic spheres constantly collide. (A more accurate, less poetic translation of Valenzuela's title, *Realidad nacional desde la cama,* is "National Reality as Perceived from the Bed.") The *Señora* feels alone and aloof. Indeed, at one point she tells Doctor Alfredi: "I feel as if someone was trying to wipe my memory clean, I don't know, oblit-erate it with new inscriptions. I don't understand it at all." To which he answers: "That happens a lot here. What else is worrying you?" Similar sarcastic comments on Argentine psychology—like the one suggesting that the country is the best on earth, even if the rest of humankind re-fuses to accept it—constantly emerge. By the book's end, a military ma-neuver, at once ridiculous and explosive, shaped to save the nation's collective soul, takes place in the deceptive abyss where imagined and sensory perceptions meet. Talk about a passion for ambiguity. Valenzuela belongs roughly to the generation of Marcos Aguinis, Fernando Sorren-tino, Liliana Heer, and Ricardo Piglia; most have lived abroad, some per-manently, and have taught at American universities. Their fiction is marked by the intense desire to understand the impact of torture, xeno-phobia, and exile on Argentine society.

Valenzuela's literary career began at an early age; she wrote for peri-odicals such as *El Hogar,* a women's magazine where Borges had a col-umn. (She is the daughter of writer Luisa Mercedes Levinson, who is responsible for a much-anthologized jungle story, "El abra," and was one of Borges's female collaborators.) Encouraged by her mother, she left Argentina to gain perspective. Paris was her first stop, and in 1965, while

working for Radio Television Française, she began to feel attracted to
the short story as a literary genre, where I believe, much like Cortázar,
she excels. She returned to Argentina and worked as a journalist, only to
leave again in 1969, this time for the United States. Interest here in the
Latin American literary boom was in its early stages: Cortázar's *Hopscotch* had appeared a few years before; *One Hundred Years of Solitude*
was soon selling like hot cakes; and Borges, thanks to the International
Publisher's Prize he shared with Samuel Beckett, was newly translated
into a dozen languages and quickly becoming a classic. Valenzuela
dreamed of entering this male club and succeeded in a bit more than a
decade.

Valenzuela was ultimately disturbed by the existence she led, though.
Much like the *Señora,* she found herself in New York, dreaming in English, and felt unhappy. She returned to Buenos Aires but soon realized
the city belonged to her no more. It now belonged "to violence and state
terrorism," and she "could only sit in cafés and brood." She would spend
hours with a cup of coffee, "responding to the general paranoia and fear,
and thinking that I should write indecipherable so that nobody could
read over my shoulder. (The writer as witness? The writer as antenna?)"
Bedside Manners mirrors that troublesome return home. Whereas elsewhere in her work, including *Other Weapons, The Lizard's Tail,* and *Open
Door,* violence and death are linked to myth and erotic rituals, here the
plot is straightforward and doesn't call for deep interpretations. In Margaret Jull Costa's remarkably smooth translation (with British spellings
left intact by the publisher), the novel reads like a diary on the struggle
to adapt to life in a new milieu. "This new city isn't the one I used to
know, they've changed everything," she tells Lucho. "Now I don't know
who the enemy is, I don't know who to fight against. Before I went away
I did, now the enemy's no longer there, or at least he says he isn't, but he
is and I just don't know where I stand."

Indeed, the quote embodies Valenzuela's present existential dilemma,
and that of many members of her generation. While she's already part
of an essential chapter in Latin American letters, one in which politics
and repression metamorphosed into magical fiction, her current stand-
ing poses a challenge she's struggling to meet: how to address political
issues in the Southern Hemisphere at a time when, happily, they are less

than life-threatening. Should the region's writers become sheer entertainers, as are the majority of U.S. literati? Her younger peers such as Ana María Shúa, also influenced by Cortázar, are already exploring and exploiting new venues, signaling a way out of the current literary crisis. Which brings me back to Fuentes's cryptic metaphor at the outset of this review: Valenzuela's opulent, baroque crown and naked feet can be interpreted in numerous ways, including, prophetically, the one suggesting that her adorned style hides a certain vulnerability to new terrain. This onetime heiress of Latin American fiction appears disoriented, perhaps no longer certain who the enemy is or what to fight against—or indeed, what literature is to be if not a fight.

[1995]

HOW HISPANICS BECAME BROWN

By an act of sheer misrepresentation. A loss in translation. To begin, Hispanics are a colorful bunch, a potpourri. They are not an ethnically homogeneous group, neither black nor white, and certainly not brown. What they are is a gathering of disparate people, most of which are Spanish-speakers. In an overly radicalized climate such as ours, though, the trap is obvious: since "nonnative English-speaker" equals "colored" and "colored" means "handicapped," it follows that Hispanics are all in the same low social strata, in desperate need of help. Many of them are, indeed, in and outside the United States, but not because they are uniformly colored. In fact, when talking about Hispanics in general (that is, Latin Americans and Latinos), no matter what the subject matter is, one maxim must always be remembered: class, and not race, is the defining social category.

> Are we Europeans? So many copper-colored faces
> deny it! Are we indigenous? Perhaps the answer is
> given by the condescending smiles of our blond
> ladies. Mixed? Nobody wants to be it, and there are
> thousands who would want to be called neither
> Americans nor Argentineans. Are we a nation? A
> nation without the accumulation of mixed materials,
> without the adjustment of foundations?—*Domingo
> Faustino Sarmiento*, Diario (1883)

> Mexicanos will tell you they are all one—"*¡Puros
> Mexicanos!*" But as in the United States, not all are
> equal in the eyes of justice, education and economic

opportunity. *¡En México no hay racismo!* Too many
Mexicans will tell you and insist it is classism. *¡Es la
clase y la pobreza!* Yes, you become more class
conscious in Mexico, but race also matters. Who
drives the taxi cabs? Who sells newspapers? Who
dresses well? Who is in military uniform?

—*José Antonio Burciaga,* Drink Cultura *(1992)*

Still, a tourist crossing the Rio Grande cannot but be confronted with
an obvious question: how sharp are the racial differences in the Hispanic orbit? The answer is plain and simple: quite sharp. The ruling elite
is, and has always been, invariably white, even in utopian (or antiutopian)
regimes such as the one in Fidel Castro's communist Cuba, and the Indian and black populations are not only moneyless and weak but openly
stigmatized. But these are not the sole "colors" our tourist would see: a
fourth one, bronze, is actually the more visible, for bronze, in the words
of philosopher José Vasconcelos, is the color of mestizos, the hybrid of
European and Amerindian, and they, the mestizo people, no doubt con-
form the largest population group in the whole Hispanic map. According to the 1990 census, for every white Latin American there are seven
blacks and seventy-nine mestizos—an unbalanced equation, if there ever
was one.

Black, white, bronze: what do these colors mean? Black (*lo negro, la
negritud*) is the pigment of night: it symbolizes alienation, poverty, bar-
barism, and the language of fire. White (*lo blanco, la blancura*), in turn,
represents purity, civilization, and the language of water. It is a translucent color through which light is filtered. African slaves are black and
European landowners are white. Last but certainly not least, bronze
(*bronce, lo bronceado*): malleable, ductile, and very tenacious, the shade
of copper, a sum of variable shades. Its malleability, in fact, is the one
capable of accommodating a wide range of shades, including that of
mestizos, Amerindians, and mulattos. Bronze is white and black and
more. It the color of trans-Atlantic vessels and coinage and swords and
medals and casting bells, the color of conquest and miscegenation.

(I said before that Hispanics are a colorful bunch. Ironically, before
the arrival of the Spanish conquistadores the numerous aboriginal tribes
were, as far as we modern dwellers are able to tell, "colorless." But color-

less is not color-blind: unaware of skin differences. Color entered the picture when the word *Indian* did: by the definition of an outside observer; that is, aboriginals became Indians when Europeans described them as such, and, equally, their skin acquired a darker shade the moment those foreigners with a lighter shade stood before them. This, obviously, doesn't mean that in the pre-Columbian world human skin was translucent, but it insinuates a crucial point: the Hispanic identity is the result of foreign tourists penetrating the region and, ipso facto, establishing a system of contrasts and counterpoints. [In Latin America, Columbus day is known as *El Día de la Raza*.] Just like Adam and Eve naming the biblical objects in Paradise, newcomers in the Hispanic milieu establish intellectual and esthetic parameters: when they are short, the natives are not [they are tall]; when they are astute, the natives are not [they are dumb]; when they are white-skinned, then the natives are non-white [they are bronze]. And yet, the pre-Columbian world, one also ought to say, seems to already have been predisposed to whiteness supremacy: an messianic Aztec legend pictured the return of the god Quetzalcoatl as *lo blanco*, a bearded *white* male, an announcement that opened the door to a triumphant Hernán Cortés. Whiteness, at least in the Nahuatl imagination, was the shade of the divine spheres.)

> Then Montezuma began a very good speech, saying that he was delighted to have such valiant gentlemen as Cortés and the rest of us in his house and his kingdom. That two years ago he had received news of a captain who had come to Champotán, and that last year also he had received a report of another Captain who had come with four ships. Each time he had wished to see them, and now that he had us with him he was not only at our service but would share all that he possessed with us.
>
> —*Bernal Díaz del Castillo*,
> The Conquest of New Spain *[1684]*

> One of the signs to determine whether something is truly of God and created by His divine hand, the Apostle Saint Paul teaches, is its order and law, for everything that God creates has order and law to

> which it adheres by nature. The heavens show it in
> their cyclic movements of day and night. In no less
> fashion the elements, plants, animals, and birds reveal
> it to us, for they have not maliciously destroyed the
> law and order that God created for them. Only
> wretched man wanders outside of the law, thus
> offending God and his blessed Maker.
>
> —*Fray Juan de Zumárraga,* Christian Rule *[1547]*

By means of miscegenation, these racial ingredients, *lo negro* and *lo blanco* and *lo bronce* generated a confused and confusing nomenclature of castes: at the top were the *españoles,* obviously; they were followed by the criollos, namely Spaniards by origin but born this side of the Atlantic; then came the mestizos, a hybrid of Amerindian and Spaniard; subsequently, the *castizos,* products of mestizo-white mixture; then, the Indians, followed by cholos, a cross between mestizo and African (although in Peru, a cholo is a darker-skinned mestizo); zambos, namely the children of mixed Amerindian-African blood (in Buenos Aires they were called *chinos,* meaning Chinese); and finally, the African slaves and their American-born descendants, the mulattos. Other types were at hand, of course, wherever an extra ingredient was added, as in Brazil, with its Portuguese component: hence, the nomenclature included *mamelucos* (Amerindian-Portuguese), mulattoes (Portuguese-black), *cafusos* (black-Amerindians), and *cabras* (Portuguese-mulattos). Ascent in the social latter equalled a whitening of skin-color, a blood tie to Europe; on the contrary, descent was understood as a link to Africa and a darker pigmentation. By the same token, blacks, Amerindians, and mestizos set the tone for an overall Hispanic identity, while the white elite remained isolated in its ivory tower.

> The extermination of the Indian population [in
> Puerto Rico] couldn't of course keep aboriginal
> elements from figuring in our definition as a people,
> but it seems clear to me that their contribution to our
> Puerto Rican identity was achieved primarily by
> cultural exchange between the Indians and the other
> two ethnic groups [blacks and Spaniards], in
> particular the blacks, because Indians and blacks had

been trapped in the most oppressed stratum of the
social pyramid during the early period of colonization
and therefore had more contact with one another
than either had with the dominant Spanish group.

—*José Luis González,*
The Four-Storeyed Country (1990)

Ay ay ay, that I am kinky and pure black;
kinkiness in my hair, uncivility on my lips;
and my flat nose turns mozambique.
Negress of intact hue, I cry and laugh
the vibration of being a black statue;
a chunk of night where my white
teeth sparkle;
to be a black spike
that gets entwined to the black
and twists in the black nest
wherein the black crow lies.
Black chunk of black in which I sculpt myself.

Ay ay ay, that my statue is all black.
I am told my grandfather was the slave
to whom the master gave thirty coins.

Ay ay ay, that the slave was my father
it is my sorrow, it is my sorrow.
If he would have been the master,
it would be my shame;
for in men, just like in nations,
to be a servant means to have no rights,
to be a master means to have no conscience.

Ay ay ay, that sins of the white king
be washed away in forgiveness by the black queen.

Ay ay ay, that the race escapes from me
and towards the white race hums and flies
to sink in its clever water;
or it may be that the white one will darken in the black.

Ay ay ay, that my black race escapes
and with the white one runs to become dark;
to become the one of the future
brotherhood of America!

—*Julia de Burgos,* Roses in the Mirror *(1922)*

In 1517, the Spanish missionary Bartolomé de las Casas, taking great pity on the Indians who were languishing in the hellish workpits of Antillian gold mines, suggested to Charles V, king of Spain, a scheme for importing blacks, so that they might languish in the hellish workpits of Antillian gold mines. To this odd philanthropic twist we owe, all up and down the Americas, endless things—W. C. Handy's blues; the Parisian success of the Uruguayan lawyer and painter of Negro genre, Don Pedro Figari; the solid native prose of another Uruguayan, Don Vicente Rossi, who traced the origin of the tango to Negroes; the mythological dimensions of Abraham Lincoln; the 500,000 dead of the Civil War and its $3.3 million spent in military pensions; the entrance of the verb *to lynch* into the thirteenth edition of the dictionary of the Spanish Academy; King Vidor's impetuous film *Hallelujah*; the lusty bayonet charge led by the Argentine captain Miguel Soler, at the head of his famous regiment of "Mulattos and Blacks," in the Uruguayan battle of Cerrito; the Negro killed by Martín Fierro; the deplorable Cuban rumba "The Peanut Vendor"; the arrested, dungeon-ridden Napoleonism of Toussaint L'Overture; the cross and the snake of Haitian voodoo rites and the blood of goats whose throats were slit by the *papaloi*'s machete; the habanera, mother of the tango, another old Negro dance, of Buenos Aires and Montevideo, the *candomblé*.

—*Jorge Luis Borges,* Universal History
of Infamy *(1935)*

El negro	*The Negro*
junto al cañaveral	*beside the cane field*
El yanqui	*The yankee*
sobre el cañaveral	*above the cane field*
La tierra	*The land*
bajo el cañaveral	*beneath the cane field*
¡Sangre	*Blood*
que se nos va!	*that we loose!*

—*Nicolás Guillén,* Caña *(1930)*

Strikingly, nowhere in this nomenclature is the term *brown* (*lo café*) called upon. This is symptomatic: Brown is a dusky and gloomy and serious color. Produced by the partial carbonization of woody fiber, of roasting, of sunburnt white skin, it is the mixture of orange and black. (Or of red, yellow, and black.) In Spanish, brown is *marrón*. Or, most frequently, *café*, the color of coffee. (The word for coffee is also *café*). Fernando Ortiz, the Cuban ethnographer, once described Caribbean idiosyncrasy as a counterpoint of tobacco and sugar, *tabaco* and *azucar*, blackness and whiteness, Africa and Europe—but "brownness," in his scheme, was never in. "Tobacco and sugar were children of the Indies," Ortiz claimed.

> The contrast between tobacco and sugar dates from the moment the two came together in the minds of the discoverers of Cuba. At the time of its conquest, at the beginning of the sixteenth century, by the Spaniards who brought the civilization of Europe to the New World, the minds of these invaders were strongly impressed by these gigantic plants. The traders arriving from the other side of the ocean had already fixed the greedy eyes of their ambition on one; the other they came to regard as the most amazing prize of the discovery, a powerful snare of the devil, who by means of this unknown weed stimulates the senses as with a new kind of alcohol, the mind with a new mystery, the soul with a new sin. Tobacco is a medicinal plant but it was degraded in Europe as an instrument of crime, an accomplice of

criminals. It is male: rough and bitter and aromatic. Sugar, instead, is female, a product of human toil. It seeks the light and loves the rain and is sweet and odorless.

"Sugar cane was the gift of the gods, tobacco of the devils," he argues, "she is the daughter of Apollo, he is the offspring of Persephone."

But the Caribbean is only one of the four cardinal points of the Hispanic orbit. The contrast between tobacco and sugar is replaced for rice and beans and tortillas by the mestizo race, a mix of Spanish and Indian blood. José Vasconcelos described Mexicans and Central Americans as the cosmic race, the future inheritor of the world. Its strength comes from its hybrid color, white and black and yellow. "Its appearance might seem malleable," Vasconcelos believed, "but it will shine after being polished." As Chicana activist Gloria Anzaldúa states,

> opposite to the theory of the pure Aryan, and to the policy of racial purity that white America practices, [Vasconcelos's] theory is one of inclusivity. At the confluence of two or more genetic streams, with chromosomes constantly "crossing over," this mixture of races, rather than resulting in an inferior being, provides hybrid progeny, a mutable, more malleable species with a rich gene pool.

Neither Ortiz nor Vasconcelos talked about Hispanics as the owners of a single color, let alone be it brown. So how did Hispanics become brown? Well, actually they never did. Or at least not south of the Rio Grande.

> Visiting the East Coast or the gray capitals of Europe during the long months of winter, I often meet people at deluxe hotels who comment on my complexion. (In such hotels it appears nowadays a mark of leisure and wealth to have a complexion like mine.) Have I been skiing? In the Swiss Alps? Have I just returned from a Caribbean vacation? No. I say no softly but in a firm voice that intends to explain: My complexion is dark. (My skin is brown. More exactly, terra-cotta in sunlight, tawny in shade. I do not

redden in sunlight. Instead, my skin becomes
progressively dark; the sun singes the flesh.)

—*Richard Rodriguez,* Hunger of Memory *(1982)*

As a racial category, brownness is a United States trademark. During
the Depression, "brownies," the national media announced, were being
repatriated. The same slur was used against Pachucos during the Sleepy
Lagoon and the Zoot Suit Riots in Los Angeles: it was an affront, an
insult. Was it used even before the Guadalupe Hidalgo treaty of 1848?
Most probably. Race, after all, has always been a central factor in the
United States and in the Southwest, and brown, since time immemorial,
has been a way of defining the people that are neither white nor black:
especially Spanish-speaking mestizos, but occasionally, by comparison,
Native Americans as well. In one twentieth-century Chicano memoir
after another, from that of Ernesto Galarza to those by Anthony Queen
and Richard Rodriguez, brownness begins as an affront, an insult, a turf
delineation by non-Mexicans against their Spanish-speaking counterparts. "You brownie, you spic, you son of a bitch. . . . Get the hell back to
where you belong!"

So "brown," it seems, comes along *al cruzar la frontera,* by entering
the English-speaking habitat, the moment Hispanics become Latinos.
(Not surprisingly, it lacks an equivalent in Spanish: brown, as a social
construction, does not mean *café.*) It is, from the outset, a term pertaining to dark-skinned Chicanos. And why brown and not bronze? Well, in
the American language, bronze is too shiny, too desirable, too much the
color of power and wealth. Brown, instead, is rudimentary and flat.

> *I see in the mirror*
> *my reflection: bronzed skin, black hair*
> *I feel I am a captive aboard the refugee ship.*
> *The ship that will never dock.*
>
> —*Lorna Dee Cervantes,* Emplumada *(1981)*

PRESS: Your Honor, ladies and gentleman of the
jury. What you have before you is a dilemma of our
times. The City of Los Angeles is caught in the midst

of the biggest, most terrifying crime wave in its
history. A crime wave that threatens to engulf the very
foundations of our civic well-being. We are not only
dealing with the violent death of one José Williams in
a drunken barrio brawl. We are dealing with a threat
and danger to our children, our families, our homes.
Set these pachucos free, and you shall unleash the
forces of anarchy and destruction in our society. Set
these pachucos free and you shall turn them into
heroes. Others just like them must be watching us at
this very moment. What nefarious schemes can they
be hatching in their twisted minds? Rape, drugs,
assault, more violence? Who shall be their next
innocent victim in some dark alley way, on some
lonely street? You? You? Your loved ones? No! Henry
Reyna and his Latin juvenile cohorts are not heroes.
They are criminals, and they must be stopped. The
specific details of this murder are irrelevant before the
overwhelming danger of the pachuco in our midst. I
ask you to find these zoot-suited gangsters guilty of
murder and to put them in the gas chamber where
they belong.

—*Luis Valdez,* Zoot Suit *(1978)*

By the seventies, though, brown ceased to be an affront and was meta-
morphosed into a form of pride: "I am Chicano! I am brown!" The
Chicano movement was about self-definition and self-esteem. *Chicano,*
itself a derogatory term for decades, became desirable. A pantheon of
brown heroes, regardless of their skin-color, was institutionalized: Frida
Kahlo, Vasconcelos, Tiburcio Vázquez, José Clemente Orozco,
Cuauhtémoc, Ricardo Flores Magón, Diego Rivera, Gregorio Cortes,
Emiliano Zapata . . . all Mexicans, most of them frontier folks. Since the
Civil Rights movement made race a dividing line between the haves and
have-nots, Mexican-Americans embraced the brown ticket: they became
La Raza, an appellation inspired by Vasconcelos's concept of "the cos-
mic race." Brown: this was the color of the lost desert land, of the mythi-
cal Aztlán, of the heat and anger against colonization, the color of

buffaloes ("the animal that everyone slaughters"), of the controversial *La Raza Unida Party*, which attempted to achieve, by electoral means, the overall objectives of the Chicano movement. Brown was the color of the Brown Berets, a paramilitary group formed in 1967, sponsored by an interfaith church organization and modeled after the Black Panthers and the Puerto Rican Young Lords. Brown, brown, brown . . . marches in California, Colorado, Arizona, Texas, and New Mexico, led by César Chávez, Dolores Huerta, Reies López Tijerina, and others, had brown motifs. . . . The whole Spanish-speaking Southwest became brown.

We, the people of La Raza, have decided to reject the existing political parties of our oppressors and take it upon ourselves to form *La Raza Unida Party* which will serve as a unifying force in our struggle for self-determination.

We understand that our real liberation and freedom will only come about through independent political action on our part, independent political action of which electoral activity is but one aspect, means involving La Raza Unida Party at all levels of struggle, in action which will serve to involve and educate our people. We recognize that self-determination can only come about through the full and total participation of La Raza in the struggle.

—*Ricardo Santillán, Los Angeles (1973)*

I am against discrimination . . . all of it. You say you are too. . . . Yet you speak of the white and the non-white vote. What you really mean is the Negro and the non-Negro vote. You are spending the majority of your time, money and labor on the Negro vote. You will continue to do the same. . . .

How about us who are neither white nor non-white? That is, who shall represent us who are neither Negro nor white?

There are too many people in this world who view life this way. No one ever really thought that Lincoln

or the Civil War cleared the mess up, but those of us
with sufficient intelligence, awareness and
sophistication hoped these generalizations would
soon dissipate themselves with the 1960s.

I hear you tell the Negro ministers that the whole
thing depended on them. . . . Jesus, man, how do you
swallow this! You said afterwards that this was
political expediency. Do you think they, the ministers,
thought that? Isn't this merely furthering the thing all
intelligent people are trying to kill?

It is the same with the whole party. When you speak
of civil rights, civil liberties, etc., you think of black vs.
white. When there's talk of investigation of these
rights, of federal grants for education, of cheap
housing, in other words, discrimination, you speak of
Negroes. At the Chinese banquet, when all the big
Whigs got up to talk, they mentioned first Negroes,
then Chinese. . . . And that's the way it goes. All
America is divided into three parts: white, black and
yellow. . . . How about me?

—Oscar "Zeta" Acosta, Letter
to Willie L. Brown, Jr. *(circa 1970)*

For a while the term appeared to have an aura of possibilities: by
designating themselves brown, Chicanos, to help dismantle American
notions of racial distinction, acted as a sort of third term. But the
country simply expanded to include this term as a rigidly defined pole.
. . . And Chicanos got lost: lost in a black-and-white screen. (Figura-
tively, "to do brown" is to deceive, to take in.)

The Civil Rights era gave way to the Affirmative Action craze, one in
which it is useful to lump "colored people" into a single group. Since
Chicanos were brown, by inference so were Cubans, Puerto Ricans, Dominicans, Colombians, et cetera. Brown became a synonym of both
"colored" and "Hispanic." This, of course, in spite of the fact that Cuban-
Americans are mostly white-skinned, and most Puerto Ricans are . . .
well, white and black and brown. By the late eighties and early nineties,
Chicanos themselves began to feel uncomfortable with the term *brown,*
but it was too late: it had stuck in the American imagination and since

race is everything, brownness is irreversible. Consequently, a white-skinned Argentinean in Chicago is brown, and so is a Peruvian cholo in Brownsville and a black Panamanian in Cincinnati. So *viva la simplificación!* All Latinos are now brown! No, wait: actually, not only all Latinos but all Hispanics, regardless of where they live. So take out your brown crayon and paint your Latin American map single-handedly: brown, brown, brown.

> "We do not know how to say *no,* and we are
> attracted, unconscious, like a hypnotic suggestion, by
> the predominant *sí* of the world of thought. . . .

—*René Marqués,* The Docile Puerto Rican *(1976)*

The whole affair, regardless to say, is but a misrepresentation, a loss in translation. Hispanics are not homogeneously a "colored people"; they never were and never will be. In fact, history establishes their reluctance to define themselves by the race card. Race matters, obviously, but class serves as the paradigm in Latin America. When they do otherwise, as was the case of the Chicano Movement, the result is decidedly mixed: they get lost in other people's fights. No: Hispanics are a mixed-color bunch, a hodge-podge. In any order you put it, they are European and African and mestizo, white and black and bronze . . . a kaleidoscopic mirror. They cannot escape being chastised as brown, but they do well when they don't fall into this racial trap, when they laugh at it and say *no.*

[1997]

MELODRAMA A LA CUBANA

Cristina García's second novel, *The Agüero Sisters,* is a magisterial melodrama. Its plot contains everything from fraternal rivalries to pregnant daughters at odds with their mothers, from unexplained murders to illegitimate children seeking to unravel their obscure origins—a family feud of heroic proportions. In fact, one could easily confuse it all with the latest prime-time *telenovela* on Univisión, except that García has no orchestral music interspersed, of course, nor does her book contain commercial interruptions. And she also has an astonishing literary style and a dazzling attention to detail totally alien to the world of soap operas. But her universe is ruled by radical emotions all the same and it borders on *ersatz.*

At the heart of *The Agüero Sisters* is a Cuban lineage spanning the whole twentieth century and globetrotting from Europe to the United States and back to the Caribbean basin. Ignacio Agüero, the family patriarch, is a renowned biologist. The novel opens as he kills his estranged wife, Blanca, while on a collecting trip to the Zapata Swamp, on the banks of the Río Hanábana. Pretending it was either a suicide or an accident, he carries her seventeen miles to the nearest village and, as stated by the novel's all-too-lucid omniscient narrator, he begins to tell his lies. To enhance the collision of emotions such an event precipitates, García reverts to a narrative marked by its counterpoints: using a Faulknerian style, she shifts scenes and subplots from this character to the next, from one viewpoint to another—from Constancia, the oldest Agüero sister, to her second husband, Heberto Cruz, a counter-revolutionary plotting another Cuban invasion like the one at the Bay of Pigs; from Reina, Constancia's younger sister, to her estranged daughter, Dulce Fuerte, and her own estranged husband, Gonzalo, himself Heberto's brother . . . and so on. The effect is that of a *telenovela:* we witness many lives at once, and as the various storylines unfold, each crashes against and redeems the others. This allows García to play a fascinating game of light and shadow, using one character to explain another and vice versa. A quote from early on in the novel:

> Constancia pulls her husband to the dance floor. He is diminutive, like her, and she is dressed in white, like him. Together they look like a first communion date. Heberto is a good dancer, but often reluctant. Constancia is not, but excessively enthusiastic. She lurches too far to the right on a turn, but Heberto reels her in with a practiced air. Then he steadies her with a palm to the small of her back and leads her across the room.

The result is a symphony of voices gravitating around a solar star, Ignacio Agüero. His personal diary, in fact, functions as a palimpsest of sorts: the whole family secret is hidden in it, and to bring the truth to light, various characters have to hide it first and then unearth it. This, obviously, is a structure as old as the novelistic genre itself, but in the baroque world of Hispanic America it has become a recurrent artifice, probably because of the collective urge to return, time and again, to the historical wound that lies at the origin of everything. Not that in García it feels artificial. The problem, nevertheless, is that it isn't anything altogether new either. Truly, much of what *The Agüero Sisters* delivers feels like a hand-me-down: sisters crisscross partners, santeros unite the spiritual and the earthy, and Cuba is portrayed not as one nation but two: Fidel's and everyone else's.

So what if it is derivative? my reader might ask. How much in contemporary art and literature isn't? Furthermore, isn't that the nature of melodrama—to repeat, to repeat, to repeat? Sure, and García brilliantly captures the cultural temperament. Always in search of something new, Constancia opens Cuerpo de Cuba, a beauty factory in Miami, and becomes a millionaire. As the novel progresses, she leaves the United States for Cuba, where her father's diary lies buried. Meanwhile, Reina, her sister, oscillates in the opposite direction. Sick and tired of Cuban so-

cialism, she moves to the United States and becomes Constancia's confi-
dante. Itinerant moving, indeed, is constantly taking place: New Yorkers
move to Florida, Cubans to Spain and the United States, Miamians to
Cuba—a never-ending rotation that symbolizes the ongoing Cuban exile. Nothing is static; life has a tendency to repeat itself . . . to repeat
itself.

Therein lies my problem, though. With only a slightly different approach, García already gave her readers this material, for while the bulk
of *The Agüero Sisters* takes place in 1991, as a group of Cuban counter-
revolutionaries plan to overtake Havana, it unfolds in just the same time-
frame and fashion, give or take a few years, as her debut novel, *Dreaming
in Cuban,* also about what else but sibling rivalries and counter-revolu-
tionaries and the crossroads of passion and politics. Both have the same
cast of characters and rotate around the search for clues to the family
identity. And as the genealogy is unscrambled, truth becomes increasingly foggier. "It's all a mock history," Reina whispers at one point in *The
Agüero Sisters,* and a bit later Constancia concludes: "Knowledge is a
kind of mirage," a statement well suited for her precursor, the protagonist of García's first novel.

Don't get me wrong: García is an immensely talented young Cuban-
American writer (she was born in 1958). I loved *Dreaming in Cuban*
when it was first published in 1992: it was original and endearing, and
while some accused García of misrepresenting the Afro-Cuban tradition, I embraced the book for addressing admirably what José Martí
once called *las dos Cubas,* both from within and from without. Melodrama it was, sure, but it had much more to it than laughter and Kleenex.
Its sentimentalism, it seemed to me, was well under control. And if the
behavior of any of the main characters appeared contrived, it wasn't the
writer's fault. What is reality in the Hispanic world, after all, if not an
overbearing yet hypnotizing *telenovela*?

But half a decade later, I cannot but feel that García herself has forced
a rereading of her book upon me. My feelings toward *The Agüero Sisters*
are complex, and thus my ambiguity toward her whole novelistic enter-
prise. With her second title, I think, she has accomplished what appears
to be almost impossible: she has rewritten the exact same book twice.
Not word by word, like a Pierre Menard rewriting *Don Quixote* in the

style of French symbolism, but through mimicry. She has become her own imitator, possibly even surpassing her own early achievement. *The Agüero Sisters* is indeed a wonderful book, but not a wonderful *second* book. It returns to the same ground of its predecessors without taking any risks, without expanding into new horizons. Its prose is stupendous, its characters well-rounded. But it is also predictable simply because García has already prepared us for this kind of structure and plot. So much so that the excellence of *Dreaming in Cuban* is suddenly lessened by its author showing us the props and strings of its melodramatic structure. Not that I would rank her alongside Corín Tellado, the father of all Spanish-speaking melodramatists: García's imagination is a treasure box of possibilities. So I do feel disappointed that she has not dared to explore new structures and techniques, to reinvent herself anew as an artist. This makes me invoke a fastidious but memorable drama teacher I once had, whose credo was "Don't give your audience what it requests, but teach it to want more."

Melodrama has the habit of infiltrating serious literature everywhere, of course, but among Latinas of García's generation this habit appears to be more accentuated. The reason, perhaps, is the overwhelming emphasis Hispanic civilization places on emotions and the unparalleled influence soap operas have played in it since the fifties, particularly among women. Theirs is a universe where passion reigns and everyone is vulnerable and peevish and a bit insincere. García surely isn't the sole explorer of the *telenovela* qua literary form—but she is one of the most gifted. Is she a risk-taker though? Is she capable of other forms of narrative? Should we expect to be surprised in a writer's second act? Well, if not surprised, at least amazed by his or her courage. *The Agüero Sisters* is about revenge and love and hatred and especially about courage—courage in all its forms: courage to antagonize a regime, courage to leave one's wife, courage to be reconciled with one's own past. Ironically, what the novel lacks is García's courage to show other facets of her writing self—not more of the same but the same in another vessel.

[1997]

INDEX

Acosta, Oscar "Zeta," quoted, 145–46
Agüero Sisters, The (García), 148–51
Ahí está el detalle (film), 46–47,49
Alfau, Felipe, 86, 118
Anzaldúa, Gloria, quoted, 142
Arau, Alfonso, 94–95, 97, 112–13
Arenas, Reinaldo, 105–6
Argentina, writers from, 129–34
Around the World in Eighty Days (film), 49
Arroyo, Antonio Vanegas, 68
Aura (Fuentes), 59
Avellaneda, Alonso Fernández de, 122–24

Bedside Manners (Valenzuela), 131–32
Before Night Falls (Arenas), 105–6
Belascoarán Shayne, Héctor (PITII character), 25–29
Bonfil, Carlos, 50
Borges, Jorge Luis, quoted, 140
Brecht, Bertolt, quoted, 123
Breton, André, quoted, 73
Bronze Screen, The (Fregoso), 45
brown, Hispanics as. *See* race
Buffalo Nickel (Salas), 120–21
Buñuel, Luis, 48–49
Burciaga, José Antonio, quoted, 135–36
Bush, George H., 6

Cabio, Juan Carlos, 104
calaveras, 68–69
Calvino, Italo, 79
Canclini, Néstor García, on *rascuachismo,* 33
cantinfladas, 39–41, 45–47
Cantinflas, 38–40, 47–52; comic style of, 43–47; influence of, on Hispanic art, 37–38, 40–43; obscurity of, 34–37
Cantinflas: Aguila o Sol (Bonfil), 50
Cárdenas, Lázaro, 51
Castañeda, Jorge, 93
castes. *See* race
Cerda, Martha, 76–80
Cervantes, Lorna Dee, quoted, 143
Cervantes Saavedra, Miguel de, 122–24
Chaplin, Charlie, compared to Cantinflas, 38, 43–45
Charlot, Jean, 33, 70–72
Chicano movement, 144–47
Chinchachoma, Padre, 23–24
Cisneros, Sandra, 81–87, 119; quoted, 82
"colored people." *See* race
Color Purple, The (Walker), 85
Cortázar, Julio, 130
Cuba: gay community in, 103–8; writers from, 118, 148–51
cursi, described, 31–32

Danzón (film), 96
de Burgos, Julia, quoted, 139–40
Delgado, Miguel M., 40
detective novels, popularity of, in
    Mexico, 27–29
de Zumárraga, Fray Juan, quoted, 137–
    38
Díaz, Porfirio, 70, 78
Díaz del Castillo, Bernal, quoted, 137
Don Quixote de la Mancha (Cervan-
    tes), 122–24
Dr. Alt (Gerardo V. Murillo), 72
Dreaming in Cuban (García), 150–51
*Dream of a Sunday Afternoon in
    Alameda Park* (mural), 69

Eisenstein, Sergei Mikhailovich,
    Posada's influence on, 73
*El ingenioso hidalgo Don Quijote de la
    Mancha* (Avellaneda), 122–24
Elizalde, Guadalupe, 37
El Jicote (newspaper), 64, 66
El Salvador, 114–16
El Sup, 13–15; emergence of, 16–20,
    23–24; identity of, speculated on,
    20, 22–24; quoted, 17–22
Esquivel, Laura, 94–98, 109–13;
    rascuachismo of, 32

False Quixote, The (Avellaneda), 122–
    24
Ferré, Rosario, 125–28
Fields, W. C., quoted, 45
Figueroa, Gabriel, 47–48
films, Cuban, 103–8
films, Mexican, 47–49; *A Kiss to This
    Land*, 100–103; *Like a Bride*, 98–
    100; *Like Water for Chocolate*, 94–
    98. *See also* Cantinflas
Fregoso, Rosa Linda, quoted, 45
Fuentes, Carlos, 36, 57–62, 93; quoted,
    129

Galeana, Benita, 54–56
García, Cristina, 148–51
gay community, in Cuba, 103–8
Goldberg, Daniel, 100–103
González, José Luis, quoted, 138–39
Guillén, Nicolás, quoted, 141
Guillén Vicente, Rafael Sebastián. *See*
    El Sup
Gutiérrez Alea, Tomás (Titón), 103–8

Hanukkah, in Mexico, 10–12
Hasta no verte, Jesús mío (Poniatow-
    ska), 92
Hijuelos, Oscar, 117
homosexuals, in Cuba, 103–8
House on Mango Street, The (Cisne-
    ros), 82–87
House on the Lagoon, The (Ferré), 125–
    28

Ibargüengoitia, Jorge, 36
IMCINE (Instituto Mexicano de
    Cinematografia), 97
Instituto Mexicano de Cinematografía
    (IMCINE), 97

Jarry, Alfred, Posada's influence on, 66
Jews, in Mexico, 10–12, 98–103, 115–
    16
Juárez, Benito, 66
Juliá, Edgardo Rodríguez, 125

Kahlo, Frida, 53–56, 90
Kandell, Jonathan, quoted, 40
King, John, quoted, 47
Kiss to This Land, A (film), 100–103
Krauze, Enrique, 60

Labyrinth of Silence, The (Paz), 53
La carpa de los Rascuachis (play), 38
La Girlfriend. See Cisneros, Sandra
Lake Jackson (Texas), 4–5

La noche de Tlatelolco (Poniatowska), 23

La noche oscura del Niño Avilés (Juliá), 125

La Raza Unida Party, 144–45

Latino fiction, revival of, 117–21

Law of Love, The (Esquivel), 110–13

Like a Bride (film), 98–100

Like Water for Chocolate (Esquivel), 109, 112–13; film, 94–98

literatura testimonial, 92

lithography, history of, in Mexico, 66–70

Lizard's Tail, The (Valenzuela), 130

Locos: A Comedy of Gestures (Alfau), 86, 118

Los olvidados (film), 49

los tiempos de Don Porfirio, 78

MacAdam, Alfred, 114n

Macondo syndrome, the, 127–28

Madero, Francisco, 70

magical realism, 71, 85, 127–28

Magical Reels (King), 39

Mambo Kings Play Songs of Love, The (Hijuelos), 117

Manilla, Manuel, 68–69

Marcos, Subcomandante. *See* El Sup

Marihuano, Don Chepito (Posada character), 71

Mario Moreno y Cantinflas . . . rompen el silencio (Elizalde), 37

Marqués, René, quoted, 147

Márquez, Gabriel García, 127–28

Marx Brothers, compared to Cantinflas, 45

massacre, at Tlatelolco Square, 23, 36, 92, 96

Massacre in Mexico (Poniatowska), 92

Mella, Julio Antonio, 90

melodrama, 109, 148–51

Memories of Underdevelopment (film), 105

Mexican Shock, The (Castañeda), 93

Mexico: Jews in, 10–12, 98–103, 115–16; militant students in, 20–23, 36, 92, 96; womanhood in, 53–56. *See also* Cantinflas; El Sup; films, Mexican; Posada, José Guadalupe; *names of specific authors*

Mister Palomar (Calvino), 79

Modotti, Tina, 89–93

Monsiváis, Carlos, 36–37

Monterroso, Augusto, 61

Moreno, Mario Arturo, 37

Moreno Reyes, Fortino Mario Alonso. *See* Cantinflas

movies. *See* films, Cuban; films, Mexican

murals, popularity of, in Mexico, 63

Murillo, Gerardo V. (Dr. Alt), 72

Myself with Others (Fuentes), 59

National Enquirer, 8–9

Nava, Gregory, 8

Neruda, Pablo, quoted, 91–92

New Time for Mexico, A (Fuentes), 93

Novo, Salvador, 36

Olmos, Edward James, 8

Orange Tree, The (Fuentes), 58–61

Ordaz, Gustavo Días, 36

Orozco, José Clemente, Posada's influence on, 63, 69, 72–73

Ortiz, Fernando, quoted, 141–42

Partido Nacional Revolucionario, 90

Partido Revolucionario Institucional. *See* PRI (Partido Revolucionario Institucional)

Patoski, Joe Nick, 8

Paz, Octavio, 53–54, 60, 64–66

Paz, Senel, 105–6

Pedroza, Trinidad, 64

pelado, described, 48

Peña, Richard, 47
People (magazine), 7
Pepe (film), 49
Pérez, Selena Quintanilla, 3–9
PITII (Paco Ignacio Taibo II), 25–29, 93; *rascuachismo* of, 32
political cartoons, popularity of, in Mexico. *See* Posada, José Guadalupe
Ponce de León, Ernesto Zedillo, 51
Poniatowska, Elena, 23, 84, 89–93
Portugal, Jesús Gómez, 64
Posada, José Cirilo, 64
Posada, José Guadalupe, 63–66, 69–72; *calaveras* of, 68–69; *rascuachismo* of, 32–33; "rediscovery" of, 72–75
Posada: Messenger of Mortality (Wollen), 73
Posada: The Man Who Portrayed an Epoch (Rodríguez), 69–70
PRI (Partido Revolucionario Institucional): forerunner of, 90; rejection of *rascuachismo* by, 35–36
printmaking, history of, in Mexico, 66–70
Profile of Man and Culture in Mexico (Ramos), 48
Puerto Rico, writers from, 125–28

Quintanilla, Abraham, Jr., (Selena's father), 5, 8

race: distinctions in, analyzed, 135–36, 143–47; nomenclature of, 136–43
Ramos, Samuel, quoted, 48
rascuachismo: described, 32–34; metamorphosis of, 49–51; rejection of, by elite, 35–37, 51–52
Realidad nacional desde la cama. See Bedside Manners (Valenzuela)
Red Sunrise (film), 96
Rega, José López, 130

Rivera, Diego, 36, 53; Posada's influence on, 63, 69, 72; quoted, 74
Roberts, Marion, 37
Rodríguez, Antonio, quoted, 69–70
Rodriguez, Richard, quoted, 142–43

Salas, Floyd, 119–21
Saldívar, Yolanda, 5–8
Salinas de Gortari, Carlos, 51
Santillán, Ricardo, quoted, 145
Sarmiento, Domingo Faustino, quoted, 135
Schyfter, Guita, 98–100
Selena, 3–9
Selena (film), 8
Señora Rodríguez and Other Worlds (Cerda), 76–80
Siqueiros, David Alfaro, Posada's influence on, 63, 72
Strawberry and Chocolate (film), 103–8
students, militant, in Mexico, 20–23, 36, 92, 96
Suárez, Constancio, 68

Taibo, Paco Ignacio, II. *See* PITII (Paco Ignacio Taibo II)
Tattoo the Wicked Cross (Salas), 119
That's the Deal (film), 46–47, 49
Three Stooges, compared to Cantinflas, 45
Tinísima (Poniatowska), 89–93
Tin Tán, 39
Titón (Tomás Gutiérrez Alea), 103–8
Tlatelolco Square massacre, 23, 36, 92, 96

UAM (Universidad Autónoma Metropolitana), 20, 22–24
UNAM (University Nacional Autónoma de México), students at: El

Sup's response to, 20–22; massacre of, 23, 36, 92, 96

Universidad Autónoma Metropolitana (UAM), 20, 22–24

University Nacional Autónoma de México. *See* UNAM (University Nacional Autónoma de México), students at

Valdez, Luis, 38; quoted, 143–44

Valenzuela, Luisa, 129–34

Varela, Antonio, 64

Vasconcelos, José, 136, 142, 144

Villaseñor, Victor, 8, 119

Villaurrutia, Xavier, 36

Vuelta (literary magazine), 35

Walker, Alice, 85

Wollen, Peter, 68, 73

Woman Hollering Creek (Cisneros), 83–84

womanhood, in Mexico, 53–56, 110

Xochimilco campus (UAM), 20, 22–24

Ybarra-Frausto, Tomás, on *rascuachismo,* 33–34

Zapata, Emiliano, 70

Zapatistas, 16–20

Zubareff, Valentina, 40